CARRY IT BETTER

CARRY IT BETTER

Pressure, Responsibility, and Learning to Love Without Bracing

E.J. ELLSWORTH

This book is based on the author's personal lived experience and is not intended as medical, psychological, or therapeutic advice, nor does it replace professional mental health treatment. Readers seeking support should consult a qualified professional.

Individual experiences and outcomes will vary. The author and publisher assume no liability for emotional, relational, or psychological impacts resulting from applying the concepts in this book. Any reference to physical movement or exercise describes the author's personal experience only. Readers with health conditions should consult their doctor before making changes to physical activity.

The concepts discussed reflect the author's understanding of established ideas in psychology, neuroscience, and human behaviour, interpreted through personal experience rather than presented as formal academic instruction.

Some identifying details have been omitted or generalised to protect the privacy of individuals.

This book is not intended to identify, describe or comment on any specific employer, workplace, organisation, colleague, client, incident, proceeding, agreement or confidential matter. Any references to work, career, responsibility or professional environments are expressed in general terms and reflect the author's personal experience only.

Nothing in this book is intended to allege wrongdoing, fault, misconduct or responsibility on the part of any person, organisation, employer or institution.

References to books, authors, concepts or areas of research are included for general discussion and further reading only. No endorsement, sponsorship, affiliation or approval is implied.

If a reader is in immediate danger, experiencing a crisis, or believes they may harm themselves or another person, they should contact their local emergency services or a crisis support line.

ISBN 978-1-7646433-8-2 (ebook)

ISBN 978-1-7646433-4-4 (hardback)

ISBN 978-1-7646433-9-9 (paperback)

Cover, interior design and artwork by Ian Koviak.

First edition.

To my children

With love, always.

Contents

Introduction

You may be reading this from any point in your life. You may be climbing, building something, carrying more than you let anyone see. You may be stretched across a business, a family, a relationship, and a version of yourself that barely resembles the person you were before responsibility started stacking up. You may be the one everyone leans on, the one who shows up regardless, the one who holds the structure together while the pressure underneath keeps building in a way you are fully aware of but have no idea how to address.

You may be reading this in an airport lounge between flights, in a parked car before walking into the house, or at two in the morning because sleep stopped being something your body knows how to do. You may be reading this because someone handed it to you, or because the title caught you for a second and you are not sure why.

Sustained responsibility reshapes a person from the inside out, and it does so regardless of where the pressure comes from. It does not matter whether you take a demanding career path, run a company, raise children alone, or hold a family together through sheer will. The pattern is the same. The internal pace rises to meet the demand, and it stays there long enough that the elevation stops feeling temporary and settles into feeling like who you are. Patience shortens in ways that surprise you, tone shifts before you catch it, and small things land heavier than they should. The people closest to you feel the change before you do, because proximity does not protect them from what you are carrying, it exposes them to it. The gap between the person you want to be and the person who keeps showing up in pressured moments becomes harder to explain away, and you start to wonder whether the tension you feel at rest is just the way you are built.

My version of that pattern started young. I was nineteen when I walked into a career that would shape the next sixteen years of my life in ways I did not have the language or the tools to understand. It had been the dream long enough that arriving inside it felt like purpose rather than risk. The work involved sustained, repeated exposure to the kind of pressure that does not leave your body when the day ends. It lives in the sleep, in the way your chest tightens in a room that you should feel safe, in the way your mind starts scanning for threat during a quiet afternoon with your own children. Not one event and not one difficult day, but a slow compounding across years of showing up, absorbing, and moving forward, and the knowledge of how to carry that kind of accumulation without it carrying you simply did not exist in my life yet.

How a nervous system works, what sustained pressure does to a person across years of accumulation: that understanding came much later than the accumulation itself. It showed up in my relationships, in the distance that grew without either of us choosing it, in the way I was present everywhere and not fully available anywhere.

By the time my body made the damage impossible to ignore, the layering had been building across the whole of that period. Sleep had fractured into something barely functional. My startle reflex was so heightened that ordinary sounds sent adrenaline through me before I could think. Irritability sat underneath everything like a current I could not turn off. Nightmares surfaced without pattern and flashbacks arrived uninvited, triggered by faces and environments that had nothing to do with the present moment. Concentration thinned and memory shortened, and I felt sick before work, my heart pounding at my temples while I tried to hold it together on the outside. The hum I had been carrying across all of that was no longer background noise, it was running the entire system, and the system was breaking down in ways I could no longer push through.

What that looked like in my life was relationships that ended and people I loved bearing the cost of a version of me that I would not have chosen if I had known how to come down. I have a son with my first partner and a daughter with my second, and the love I felt for all of them was never in question. What I could not do was show up with the steadiness and emotional presence that love required, because I was running so elevated that the weight I carried did not stay contained inside me. It reached them, and it shaped the atmosphere they lived in. My daughter now lives on the other side of the world, and the distance between my son and his sister is something I sit with every day. I carry guilt for what my state cost the people closest to me, and I should carry it, because understanding why I was the way I was does not undo what it meant for them.

I could point at the cause and stop there, and plenty of people do. They identify what shaped them, they name the weight, and they sit inside that identification as though understanding the wound is the same as healing it. Knowing why you are wired a certain way does not unwire you, and naming the source of your reactivity does not make you less reactive. If nothing moves after the naming, all you have is a more articulate version of the same patterns playing out in the same rooms with the same people paying the cost. I wanted to change how I carried it, and that required something beyond insight.

I owned it. The pressure was real, what it did to my body and my mind was real, and so was every moment where I showed up shorter, sharper, and more compressed than the people around me deserved. I am not hiding behind what happened to me and I am not using context as a shield. What I am doing is painting it honestly so that what is in these pages makes sense, that the way I carried myself was the product of sustained load on a system that never learned how to regulate under pressure, and I take full responsibility for how that played out in every part of my life.

The rest of these pages trace the full arc of that process. The slow, invisible rise in baseline that felt like something earned, the cost that only became visible when it reached the people I loved, and the deliberate, unglamorous, repetitive work of learning how to lower it again, widen the range, and carry responsibility without bracing against every moment. I did not write this to perform healing or to present a finished version of myself.

If you are holding this book right now, you may be somewhere in that arc yourself. You might be at the beginning, where the pressure still feels manageable and the pace still feels like something you chose. You might be in the middle, where the cost is becoming harder to ignore and the gap between who you are at your best and who keeps showing up under load is widening in ways that unsettle you. You might be past the fracture, sitting in the aftermath of what sustained elevation cost you, wondering whether the damage defines what comes next. If you are there, I want you to know that I have sat in that same place, and I hope you find the support and the people who help you see that the fracture does not have to be the end of the story, the same way others helped me see that in mine. Or perhaps you may not be in it yourself and still you can see it in your partner, your friend, your colleague, someone you care about who is carrying more than they are letting on. Wherever you are reading from, something in the title or the cover or the first few pages brought you here, and that is enough of a reason to keep going.

What follows is not every story. There are moments I have not written about, conversations I have left where they happened, and parts of those years that belong to the people who lived them alongside me. The women who raised children with me carried something real through that period, and I know that what I was going through did not make it easy to be close to me. I was not the version of myself I wanted to be, and the people nearest to me felt that most. I have no interest in writing a version of events that softens what that would have felt like from where they were standing. I chose what I chose because it traces the arc honestly, not because it represents the full weight of everything they felt. A memoir is not a confession, and it is not a defence. It is a selection made with care, by someone who lived it, and what I selected is what I believe most clearly explains how a person ends up carrying more than they know how to hold.

I think about it sometimes. What if I had carried it better from the start? What if I had never taken that kind of work on, or taken it but learned how to leave it at the door? What if I had understood relationships the way I understand them now, made fewer mistakes, shown up differently in the rooms that mattered most. Would my kids be playing together every day? Would the relationships have been held? Would we all still be under the same roof? I do not know the answer to that and I never will, and I have had to make a kind of peace with the not knowing, because sitting inside that question without resolution is its own kind of sentence.

What I do know is that the realisation I arrived at is not unique to me. Relationships fracture for all kinds of reasons, in all kinds of lives, and the people inside them are usually doing the best they can with what they have been given and what they know. Everyone's pain is real. None of it is small just because someone else is carrying something too. Whatever you are carrying, it counts. It matters. And I hope that whatever it is, you find a way to carry it better.

Part One

The Baseline Shift

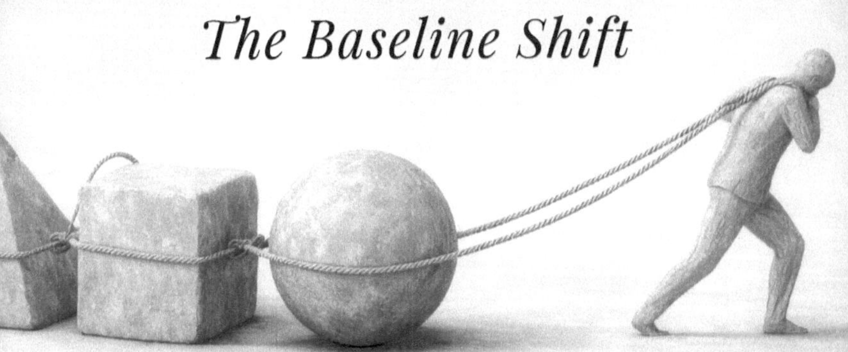

Responsibility

Everyone who has ever carried real responsibility for other people knows the moment it stops being something you do and just becomes something you are. It does not arrive with an announcement or a ceremony. You might realise it over many weeks or months, and it builds through repetition, through the daily act of showing up and being the one who holds the pieces in place, until one day you cannot remember the last time you moved through a day without tracking what someone else needed from you. It does not matter whether that responsibility came through parenthood, a business, or a career that never switches off or a combination of all of them at once. The pattern is the same. The internal pace adjusts upward to meet the demand, and it stays there, and after long enough at that level you stop noticing the elevation because it has become the only setting you know. Do not get me wrong though, some areas of life require that level of functionality, but there needs to be a way you can lower that elevation, and that's something I did not do.

I lived in that pattern before I recognised it for what it was. The beginning of it looked nothing like pressure. It looked like a good life. I spent seven years with my first partner, and for most of those years, things were easy in the way things are easy when two people have enough room around them to just exist without everything feeling urgent or in a rush. We had met through work and grown into each other over time. Weekends were ours and we went out with friends in the city, we took trips when we felt like it, and none of it required the kind of careful planning that would later dominate every corner of my life. I did not appreciate how much of that ease had to do with space, with the simple fact that neither of us was carrying enough yet for the weight to show up in how we treated each other. I thought the ease was something we had built together, when really it was something we had not yet lost.

Friday nights in the city with friends were fun, staying out late even though I knew it was way past my bedtime. Friends used to laugh if I stayed out past nine o clock (they still do). Maybe I am just an old soul. I slept well and recovered fast and whatever the week had taken out of me there was still plenty left over, and there was no reason to think at that time that anything would change.

My son was born inside that relationship, and the love I felt for him was immediate and enormous and unlike anything I had experienced before. Becoming his father gave me a sense of purpose that was more grounded and real than anything work had ever offered, and I stepped into the role with everything I had. But the reality of a newborn reorganised the mechanics of daily life and it did so at a pace that left very little room to adjust. The mornings started earlier, the nights became broken, and the weekends that had once belonged to rest and recovery filled up with routines and the sort of constant vigilance that comes with keeping a small person alive and safe. My partner and I were both in it, both exhausted, both trying to figure out how to be parents while keeping the rest of our lives from sliding. I guess I started to feel the easy space between me and my partner closing over that period. Priorities changed and it wasn't anything either of us did, I think it was just what happens when you've been running empty for too long. Fatigue like that wears on you, and I didn't know how to carry it well. Honestly, I didn't carry it well at all.

If you are reading this as someone trying to build a business while holding everything else together, or as someone who has recently become a parent, or as someone who has watched the ease in your relationship slowly give way to logistics and tiredness and a feeling that there is never quite enough of you to go around, then you already know what I am describing. You know the feeling of waking up already behind. You know what it is like to move through a day so quickly that you do not register any single part of it until you are lying in bed at night and the whole thing replays at once. When all you could think about during the day was the moment you could lay down. You know the guilt of wanting silence more than you want company, and you know how difficult it is to admit that to anyone, including yourself.

My career did not pause to make room for any of it. I was still carrying a full workload, still absorbing what each day put in front of me, still going into work on my days off because the feeling of something left unfinished just ruined any time off. The two worlds, work and family, had been separate for most of my twenties, but they were not separate anymore. Work came through the front door with me every evening, settling into my body as a tension. Fatherhood and fatigue filled all other spaces with its own legitimate demands. I could not tell which one was doing what to me on any given day because the two had merged into a single unbroken current of demand that ran from the moment I opened my eyes to the moment I closed them. I told myself this was what responsible people did, and I did not question it because everyone around me seemed to be operating the same way.

After seven years my first partner and I separated. Our son was still young enough to be in daycare. There was nothing dramatic about the ending at all. Looking back, it was just two people who drifted apart. What I will say is that my compression played its part, and I carried more of it into the space between us than I should have. The hardest thing was the parent guilt about my son now living between two houses. Shared care replaced shared living, two houses replaced one, and the weeks split into structured blocks.

On the weeks I had my son the days ran to a rhythm. Up before dawn, get him ready, daycare drop-off, then straight into whatever work had waiting for me, pickup in the afternoon, home, dinner, bath, stories, bed, and then sitting in the afterwards with the whole day still circulating through my chest and the knowledge that tomorrow would run in exactly the same sequence. Weekends I was empty and wanting to close my eyes and not be needed by anyone for a few hours. I craved silence, and the craving had nothing to do with wanting to be away from my son. My body was asking for a pause it had not had.

I soon bought an apartment and found myself in the dating scene. I moved into my next relationship without stopping. There was no deliberate decision to skip over what had happened and get straight into something new, it just felt like forward movement, the natural next thing, the way everything in my life at that point felt like the next thing that needed to happen. I processed by moving, by filling the space with whatever came next, and that was a pattern I had been running, long before I ever applied it to my personal life. I carried the same internal speed and the same unresolved load into something new, carrying everything that had built up without knowing what it would do to what I was walking into. I carried the same posture into this new relationship and she deserved someone slower and more settled than I was able to be. But I was head over heels, the feeling of that new relationship, it was like a breath of fresh air. It kind of felt like a recharge. I was no longer a single parent juggling my son, there was stability. But that stability I took for granted. I became complacent.

We built a life together over years, living together, raising my son together on my weeks, building the kind of shared routine that felt stable, grounded, and real. There were good years in it, years where the life we had looked exactly like something you would want if you saw it from the outside. I do cherish that time, it did mean a lot to me and I was so thankful that she took on the role of stepmother to my son. But I was still running at the same pace underneath all of it, and that pace does not care how good the surface looks even if you are thankful or loving or appreciative. The pace sat beneath everything and it coloured every interaction and every moment with something the people closest to you can feel even when you cannot feel it yourself.

There were evenings where the three of us sat around the table and the house felt full. My son had someone beside me who cared about him, and the life we were building looked really good. I do not hide behind that honesty because it was real.

My daughter was born about four years after my son. I loved her from the first moment, and the feeling was enormous, protective, and instinctive, surprising, even though I had been through it before. But something was different this time, and it matters for context because I want you to understand what sustained pressure did to me over the course of years, and what this effect had on me. I was there physically but something was distant between me and my daughter. I was there physically, I was present in every practical sense, but there was a gap between the love I felt and the ease I expected to feel alongside it.

While my partner was recovering in the hospital, exhausted and emotional after giving birth, I was filling out paperwork. I had the birth certificate done and the passport application lodged within a day, because that was how I operated, always moving to the next thing that could be completed, always finding something to do with my hands rather than sitting still inside a moment that was asking for something softer and slower than anything I knew how to offer. A newborn needs someone who can slow down and be fully there without reaching for the next task, and I had not operated at that speed in longer than I could remember.

I did not know how to sit inside a moment without part of me already planning what came after it, and that inability showed up in those early days with my daughter.

Those months after she was born I was carrying everything at once, and every role I held was real and deserved my full presence, and not one of them was getting it because they were all drawing from the same well inside me, and the well was empty. I thought I was there every single day for my children and for my partner, and the love I had for all of them was constant and deep and never in question, but I was moving so quickly through all of it that I was never fully inside any single part of it. The people who mattered most to me were living with the most compressed version of who I was, the version that had nothing left beyond whatever was immediately in front of it. I kept moving, because moving was all I knew how to do, and because I was afraid of what would happen to everything I was holding together if I ever let myself stop. I always wanted a daughter; it was the greatest feeling knowing she was coming. But the days, weeks and months following her birth, I found it hard to connect. I should have told my partner. I knew what the medical term for it was, but I ignored it, because it didn't align with my expectations. I don't know why I struggled with that alone, maybe it was the embarrassment of not feeling that connection, or perhaps I was worried of what people would think. In any case, I sat with it, and the gap eventually narrowed, until I felt that full connecting moment. I remember it, I was home with her whilst my partner was at work. She had just started crawling. I was on the lounge room floor with her. I picked her up as I was laying on my back and let her rest on my face. She then started to eat my nose. It's not like she hadn't done that before, babies put everything in their mouths, but this time it just felt different. It was beautiful, it was the first time I felt that true connection, even with the slobber all over my cheeks. I know that feeling came later than it should have, but it did arrive, and I'm so grateful it did. Now regardless of pressure and responsibility, I'm aware that this feeling may have occurred anyway, but I do know I wasn't myself at that time.

If you have ever held someone you love and felt something missing at the same time, if you have ever been physically present with your family while knowing somewhere in your body that the version of you in the room is not the full version you want to be, then you understand what I am describing. It is what happens when every part of your life is drawing from the same depleted place inside you and none of the people who matter most are getting what they actually need, and you can see that happening but you cannot slow down long enough to change it because the speed is the only thing keeping the whole structure upright. If I can say anything now, please slow down.

Always Ready

Other people mistake readiness for competence, and the mistake is understandable because from the outside the two look almost identical. You think ahead, you catch things before they become problems, you walk into a room and within seconds you have already assessed the dynamics and identified where the friction is likely to come from. The people around you experience that as someone who is sharp and reliable. In professional environments it earns trust and in the home it reads as diligence. What nobody sees, because the surface is so convincing, is that underneath all of it your body has not been at rest in longer than you can remember, and that the scanning and the anticipating have become a setting your nervous system locked into long ago and has not come down from since.

If you recognise yourself in that description, if you are the one in your family or your business or your team who seems to have thought of everything before anyone else has even noticed there is something to think about, I am not going to tell you that what you are doing is wrong. In many situations it serves those closest to you and keeps things running that would otherwise fall apart. I did it myself, but what I want you to sit with is whether you can turn it off when you do not need it. Whether you can walk into a room that is calm and experience it as calm, without some part of you running scenarios in the background. Whether the last time you felt fully at rest is something you can point to or something so far back it feels like it belongs to a different person.

I could not have answered that question honestly without confronting something I was not ready to confront. I had been operating in that mode for so long that it had stopped feeling like a mode and become who I was. I had built an identity around the readiness and questioning it would have meant admitting that the thing I was most relied upon for, my ability to stay ahead of everything, might be the thing that needed addressing.

During my daughter's daycare enrolment meeting, the staff member walked us through the usual information about routines and settling and daily structure. It was a quiet room, comfortable chairs, a conversation she had clearly had a hundred times before. When she asked if we had any questions I did not ask about anything the meeting had covered. I asked what emergency management plans were in place for floods and fires, how evacuation decisions would be made, and how quickly parents would be notified if something went wrong. She paused, gave a small laugh, and explained that no one had ever asked that before. She told me that the procedures were in place and that the centre met all the relevant requirements. The conversation moved on and I believed it was a perfectly normal thing to ask. It was not until much later that I understood what that moment said about where my baseline was sitting. Nothing in that room had suggested danger of any kind. No threat, no warning, no reason whatsoever for my mind to have gone where it went. It was a routine meeting in a safe suburb on an ordinary afternoon, and my brain had bypassed everything happening in front of me and positioned itself inside a catastrophic scenario that existed nowhere outside my own head. My nervous system had spent so long in an environment where threat was real and constant that it could not recognise a safe room when I was sitting inside one, and the question I asked in that meeting was my baseline talking, not my parenting. What I should have been asking was, can she bring her comforter with her, how many children are in her class, what will she be eating for breakfast and lunch. Those sorts of questions that any parent should ask. Instead, I was worried about the centre catching fire or being flooded.

That same pattern continued to show up everywhere. I would take my son for a walk and spend the time scanning the trees overhead because somewhere in my body I was convinced one of them was going to come down. I would drive to the shops and feel a low dread about hitting a pedestrian that had no basis in anything real but sat in my stomach like a fact. These thoughts arrived constantly and they always presented themselves as reasonable because they were dressed in the language of caution and care. Who argues with a thought that tells you it is trying to keep your family safe. I just absorbed them and carried them alongside everything else. Those imagined threats sat on top of the real ones until the two became indistinguishable.

Cafes were the same. I could not sit with my back to a room, and I would walk in already scanning for a table against a wall or in a corner, somewhere that gave me sightlines to the entrance and as much of the space as possible, and if the only seats available meant sitting with my back to other people I would suggest somewhere else or find a reason to get a takeaway instead. If I had no choice I would eat quickly and leave, my shoulders carrying a low readiness the whole time that had nothing to do with getting a coffee. I was never fully in the room the way the other people in it appeared to be, settled into their chairs, leaning toward whoever they were with, their bodies telling them nothing was required, while mine was running a constant low scan of every person who came through the door.

Nobody saw any of that from the outside. I was just someone who liked a corner table. My hands moved constantly, tearing napkins, straightening cutlery that was already straight, turning my phone face down and then face up again.

I was running at a frequency that did not have an off switch, and my body did the only thing it knew what to do with the surplus, which was to move.

That is what a raised baseline looks like when it follows you into a life that has nothing to threaten you. Just a man checking his mirror on the way home and choosing his seat carefully in every café he ever walked into, the sensible behaviour of someone who pays attention, which is exactly how it presented itself to me. I carried all of it without question, and no one around me had any idea how much of my attention was being consumed by a threat that existed only inside my own nervous system. No wonder I arrived places already exhausted. The journey there had already cost me something before it had even begun. I used to wonder why whenever there was a social event, or an outing, I would get this sudden overwhelming tiredness on that particular day before the event had even started, and it's pretty clear why.

The cycle I have been describing had been running in me that it was now my identity. Sustained pressure from my career, parenthood, relationships and the accumulated weight of everything I was carrying raised my internal baseline to a level my body accepted as normal. That raised baseline compressed the range I had available for my partner, my children, anyone close, so my responses were faster and sharper than the moment required. Because I was still functioning, still showing up, still holding the structure together from the outside, I kept going. And the going fed the pressure back into the system, and the whole thing looped again. It ran without interruption. Nothing broke visibly enough to make me stop. Sure there was moments where I thought wow you could have handled that better, but the structure looked solid from the outside so I remained complacent that nothing would go wrong. If you have lived with someone who carries that gap, if you are the partner or the child of someone who is brilliant under pressure and hard to reach on an ordinary evening, I want you to know that the gap comes from what sustained responsibility does to the body. The person carrying it often can see it better than you can. In my situation I could see it clear as day, I was aware of it, but I did nothing about it. I knew I was elevated most of the time. I knew that little things irritated me that shouldn't have, but I kept telling myself to keep going. What I should have said to myself was slow down.

Sundays

I could feel it in my body every day, the weight of everything I was holding without being able to do anything about it. Work had not slowed down or become any easier to leave at the door. The hours outside of work were divided between the kids and everything else that needing holding. I went to bed still processing everything, and I woke up most mornings, exhausted but still needing to move like it was the most urgent thing to do. Sitting in bed with a hot cup of tea, that wasn't me. I had to be out the door, yet at the same time

I always thought how nice that would be to just sit still and wake up.

I could feel that something was off. It was there when I woke up, a readiness in my chest. It was there in the evenings when the kids were in bed, the house was quiet, and I could not settle into that because I did not know what to do without demand. I couldn't sit still and watch a show, without having to check the washing machine or unstack the dishwasher. If I finished a drink, the cup would immediately return to the kitchen sink. I knew the pace I was living at was not right, the same way you know you are not sleeping enough, a background awareness that never quite reaches the level of action because the thing causing the problem is also the thing you believe is holding everything together. I was aware and the awareness changed nothing; it just sat there underneath everything with nowhere to go. I guess that's worse than being naive. The only naive thing about me was thinking everything would be ok.

Even before my daughter was born, the evidence arrived every second Sunday, and it arrived in my body before it arrived in my thinking. My son would go to his moms for the week. The bags would go in the car, the front door would close, and the house would settle into a specific kind of calmness, a whole week ahead with no one in it who needed me to be switched on. In those first few minutes after the door closed my body would do something I had no say in. My shoulders would drop and my breathing would change, deeper and slower than it had been in days. I would feel something lift. It was as if I had just carried something heavy and put it down, and the calm that followed was more complete than anything I experienced at any other point during that period of my life.

I hated it because I loved my son and I missed him before the car had turned the corner, and yet my body was telling me something that felt like the opposite of what a loving father should feel. I asked myself what kind of man feels steadier when his child leaves the house, and the answer I kept arriving at was one who does not have what it takes. I believed that because it confirmed a fear I was already carrying that I was not enough for the people who needed me. I carried the guilt into the next week alongside everything else, where it added to a load that was already more than I could sustainably hold, and the added weight made the following Sunday drop even more pronounced, and around it went.

What I could not hear was that the release had nothing to do with my family or how much I loved them. It had everything to do with what I had been carrying around them; the weight of work layered on top of sustained pressure at a level my body was never meant to hold indefinitely. The Sunday changeover was the only moment in my routine where the demand paused long enough for my system to reveal what it had been holding, and I read that revelation as a failure of love when it was evidence of a baseline sitting too high.

The pattern repeated every second week. A good week, one where my son and I had spent real time together and everything had felt close to what I wanted fatherhood to look like, ended with the same physical drop as a week where I had been stretched thin and aware the whole time that I was coming up short. The drop was identical regardless, which meant it was about the state I was living in permanently, and the changeover was simply the only gap in the routine wide enough for that state to become visible.

Loving someone and having the capacity to be fully present with them are not the same thing. That cost me more than I expected. I loved my children completely, I showed up every day, and I meant it every single time. But love on its own does not create capacity. Capacity is something your body either has room for or it does not, and mine did not. I could do the tasks and run the routines and keep the coordination tight. What I could not do was sit on the couch on a Wednesday evening and feel settled in my own body while I did it, and that gap was something the Sunday changeovers showed me every fortnight whether I wanted to see it or not.

What I was feeling on those afternoons was relief. My shoulders dropped, my breathing slowed, and for a few hours the weight of the week lifted and I mistook the lightness for something lasting. But the lightness only existed because the weight had been temporarily removed. I was not at peace. Peace would have meant sitting on that couch with my son beside me and feeling settled in my own body while I did it, being in the room with the people I loved without it costing me something just to be there. I was nowhere near that, and every Sunday my body tried to show me, and every Monday I went back to the same pace as though the lesson had never happened.

I carry regret about those times. What was missing was the capacity to hold everything I was responsible for without it spilling into the atmosphere around the people I loved, and on those Sunday afternoons my body was telling me that clearly while I spent so long looking the other way. The distance between where I was and where I needed to be was growing with every repetition, and it was not going to close on its own no matter how long I waited, and that is something I know now with a certainty that cost me more than I wish it had.

I knew what was happening and I carried past it every time because I did not have the tools to do anything else. My son deserved a father who was present when he was present, and on those Sundays I was already somewhere else before his car seat was cold. The relief was real and the love was real and they existed in the same body at the same time, and I did not know what to do with that.

I spent that period living somewhere between braced and elevated, wound up, and aware that something was wrong but still performing on the outside, still functioning on the outside, carrying a constant low-level tension that never fully released. Those Sunday afternoons were the only time my body briefly slid toward something closer to regulated, where the baseline drops enough that there is real room to breathe, holding it for hours, and climbing straight back up when the new week began. Beyond regulated there is open and present, where you are available to the people you love because your system has settled enough to allow it. I could not have imagined that place back then. I could barely feel the edge of being regulated before my body pulled me back to where it was used to being.

Part Two

When It Lands

The Room

Everything I have described had been building toward a cost I could feel approaching but could not prevent. I knew the relationship with my second partner was ending. I could feel it in the way the house had changed over the preceding months, the way conversations had shortened, the way the air between us had become something we moved through carefully, choosing words. I own my part in that. The version of me she was living with was not the version she had signed up for, and I had carried the heaviness of what I was dealing with into our home. The ending had been forming for months, and by the time it became something that could not be repaired the question was no longer whether it would end, but how, and what it would cost the people who had no say in any of it.

My son was five. He was sitting on the lounge watching television on an ordinary afternoon, and he had no idea what was coming. I had been carrying the knowledge of what I needed to tell him for days, and the weight of it was different to anything my career had ever asked me to hold, because this was not someone else's crisis that I could process and hand over and move on from. The person it was about to land on was my child, and there was no version of what I was about to say that would not hurt him.

I pressed pause on the remote and sat down beside him. He looked at me the way children look at their parents when nothing has gone wrong yet, open, and calm and trusting that whatever comes next will be safe. I felt my throat close before I started speaking. I said, "Buddy, I need to tell you something," and I watched his face change before I had finished the sentence because children do not need to understand the words to know that something is about to break. They read it in your voice. He knew before I told him.

I explained that his sister and his stepmom were leaving. I do not remember the exact words I used because I was trying to hold myself together while saying them, and most of my energy was going into keeping my voice steady enough that he would not see how much of me was falling apart on the inside. His lips pouted first, then his eyes filled, and then he asked me in the most innocent breaking voice "why?" There was no anger in it, no accusation, just confusion, the kind of pure bewildered hurt that does not belong anywhere near a five-year-old, and the sound of his voice cracking on that single word is something I carry with me to this day. It landed in my heart like something permanent. His whole body seemed to register what was happening before his mind had any way of making sense of it, and all I could do was sit beside him and tell him it had nothing to do with him and that I was sorry.

He did not know about any of what had been building inside me. He did not know that his father had been running at a pace that left no room for the people he loved most, or that the weight from everything else that had been compressing the life we shared into something that could no longer hold. He only knew that the people in his house were not going to be in his house anymore, that his sister and stepmom were leaving, that his world was being pulled apart in the space of a conversation he had not asked for and could not possibly understand. I watched him try to hold it, this enormous thing that had just been placed on a body far too small for it, and the grief I felt in that moment was unlike anything I had experienced. I had seen suffering in my life, and I learned to absorb it and keep functioning, even when the functioning was its own kind of damage. But watching my own child break in front of me because of decisions I had been part of making was something no amount of professional composure could hold at a distance. I felt his pain as though it were inside my own body, and more than guilt I felt the overwhelming need to take as much of it from him as I possibly could.

I held him for a long time after that. His breathing was uneven against my chest, catching and releasing the way a child breathes when crying has not finished with them yet, and I stroked his hair and said nothing because there was nothing I could say that would make it smaller. He fell asleep against me and I did not move. I sat there with his breathing against me and the house quiet around us.

My daughter would be leaving the country in a matter of days. My son was about to lose his sister from his daily life, and I was losing my partner and my daughter at the same time. I could feel my grief sitting underneath his, both of us in the same room processing the same fracture from completely different places, him feeling it and not understanding it and me understanding it without being able to make it smaller for him. I have sat with the memory of that afternoon more times than I can count, and it has not softened. The image of his face changing, the sound of his voice breaking, the way his eyes filled while he looked at me for reassurance I could not fully give. Those things live inside me permanently and they should because that afternoon was the clearest and most painful evidence I had ever received that the way I had been carrying everything was not just affecting me. It was reaching the people who trusted me most, and the smallest of them was sitting beside me on a couch asking me why his world was falling apart.

I had known the pace was too high and the baseline was elevated and the compression was spilling into the lives of those closest to me. But knowing something without seeing its consequence is easy to live with. You can carry that kind of awareness indefinitely without acting on it if the cost stays in the background where you do not have to look at it directly. That afternoon the cost sat beside me with tears running down its face and I did not have an answer that would make it better.

What was left was a father who could see the full cost of his pace on the person he should have protected. My son did not need an explanation and he did not need a plan. He needed me to be in the room with him and feel what he was feeling and not try to make it go away. I had never done that before. I had spent my whole adult life fixing things and solving things and moving things forward, and in that room there was nothing I could do except be in the present moment with a boy who needed his dad.

What I knew in the days that followed was that I could not undo any of it but I could stop adding to it. I could be his father in a way I had not been able to be while everything was running at the speed it had been running at. I put my phone in a drawer when he was with me instead of keeping it beside me on the couch where it pulled my attention away from him every few minutes. I sat with him when he talked to me instead of half listening while I planned what needed to happen next. I got down on the floor with him when he was playing instead of watching from the other side of the room while my mind ran through the planning of the week ahead. I stopped filling every silence with a task and started letting the silence just be what it was, two people in a room together without anything needing to happen. My body still wanted to move, still wanted to reach for the next thing, still defaulted to the operational pace it had been locked into for so long. But I could feel the difference in him when I managed to slow down, the way he leaned into me more, the way his conversations got longer when he could feel that I was there and not performing being there. He needed me to be present, and present was the thing I was only just learning to offer him.

I had not rebuilt anything yet. I had not done the work that the later chapters of this book describe. I was a man standing in the wreckage of what sustained pressure had cost him, looking at his son and understanding for the first time that the cost was never going to stay contained inside me no matter how much I believed I could absorb it on my own. My daughter would be gone in days. I could feel another layer of loss approaching like something physical, and I did not know what it would do to me when it arrived. But I understood something now that I had not understood before, which was that the cost of carrying it the way I had been was no longer staying inside me, it was reaching those I cared about. And if nothing else in my life was going to make me change how I carried it, that would certainly be a reason to.

That Morning

The flight was booked and the distance had a departure date, and what was coming fell physically in my chest. I loved my daughter and the thought of her being on the other side of the world was something I could not sit with for more than minutes at a time without my body reacting to it. Her mother's family was overseas, and her support network was there, the people who had known her from the beginning. That is not to say she had no support here, because she did, but the relationship had ended and she had no family of her own in this country, and I had already seen what splitting a child between two houses does to a young life. I had watched my son move between two homes and felt the burden of what that structure asked of him, and the thought of putting my daughter through the same thing when there was an alternative that could give her and her mother real stability and security was something I could not justify no matter how much I wanted her close. If she went home, she would be stepping into something already established, something that could hold both while the dust settled. I was torn. It is difficult to explain unless you have had to weigh your own need to be near your child against what you believe is best for them, and I went back and forth on it more times than I can count.

I wrestled with it because part of me wanted to fight for proximity at any cost. But there was a harder question underneath that impulse and it humbled me every time I sat with it honestly. Was I holding on because it was best for her, or because

I could not bear the consequence of distance. I knew I could raise my daughter and I knew I would love her fiercely and that was never the doubt. The doubt was whether keeping her close would be about what she needed or about what I could not face losing. I chose what I believed would create the most immediate stability for her, and I chose it knowing it would cost me. Whether I got every part of that decision right is something I still sit with. There is regret in me and there is also understanding of the man I was in that moment, carrying guilt and trying to choose what was kind over what was comfortable. The cost would reach further than I could see, because she would be separated from her brother, from her grandparents, from routines that had already formed around her, and I could not grasp the full weight of that from where I was standing. Would I have made a more calculated decision from where I stand today? I think that's clear. But I made that decision, at that time, in the capacity I had.

The flight was early, six in the morning. I did not sleep the night before and I did not go to the airport, because I knew watching her go through those departure gates would break me. It wasn't like I dismissed the moment. I had spent the last week with her and her mother, saying goodbye, trying to come to terms with what was about to happen. That morning, instead, I went down to the beach before dawn because I knew the flight path would cross overhead, and I stood there watching the sky towards the airport waiting for it. The plane came through broken cloud and there was a moment where the full silhouette of the aircraft was visible, larger, and more real than I had expected, close enough to see the two engines on either side of the plane, and the clouds shifting in its wake as it moved above me. My stomach dropped, that sinking feeling that tells you this is real and it is happening and there is nothing you can do to bring it back. I watched the plane move further from me until there was nothing left of it. Just the sound of the ocean, a gentle breeze, and tears running down my face. I was standing in the place where I had always felt most calm, by the water, and I had never felt emptier. The poetic tragedy of it was not something I could ignore. This was where I first met her, years earlier.

The sand was cold under my feet when I went down to the beach afterwards. The sun had not come up properly yet and the water was grey and flat. I stood there long enough for the sky to lighten and the first joggers to appear behind me, and the waves came in and pulled back, and came in again. I had brought my daughter to this same stretch of beach when she was small enough to carry in one arm, walked along the sand with her balanced on my hip while the waves ran over our feet and she pointed at the water and laughed. I wiped my face with the back of my hand and walked to the car and sat there until I trusted myself to drive.

What became clear to me much later was that the love I felt for my daughter had been the one thing powerful enough to cut through the elevation I had been living in. When she was born, it overrode everything, this enormous force that broke through the compression where nothing else had, and yet I could not settle into it because my system had no room to hold it. The love arrived and the capacity to receive it fully was not there, and that gap is what I carried through those early months without being able to name it. Now she was on a plane to the other side of the world and the same love that had broken through when she arrived was breaking open to me from the other direction. Love was the thing strong enough to reach me in both moments, and in both moments my body did not know what to do with the size of it.

I went home and the house was different. Quiet in a way that was not going to lift. There was no task to focus on, no movement to distract me, no reason to reach for the next thing because there was no next thing. Just space, and in that space everything settled into me without anything to hold it back. Tears came without warning and my chest closed until breathing was difficult. I stood in my own house in silence and everything became clear for the first time. The pressure I had been carrying had shaped how I showed up in my relationships and how I dealt with what life asked of me and the cost of carrying it the way I had been carrying it, was standing in this house alone with my daughter on a plane to the other side of the world and my son processing a fracture I had helped create. I was broken.

The version of my life I had assumed would continue was gone. My daughter's daily presence, the shape of our family, the rhythm I had built around all of it, shifted in a matter of weeks. I was standing in the aftermath of decisions I had made and consequences I had earned. The grief was layered with love and regret, relief that she would be supported and pain that I would not be there, and it did not sit neatly inside any single feeling. I could not keep telling myself I would address things when life settled down, because life had settled down, and what it had settled into was consequence. I could not undo the distance or reverse what had fractured, but if I was going to survive what I had set in motion I had to change how I carried it. That was not a motivational thought. It was survival because all I wanted to do was give up.

None of this is exaggerated and none of it is written to make the situation sound worse than it was. I am telling you what happened because it is what happened, and because I think the distance between a life that looks like it is holding together and a morning like the one I have just described is shorter than I ever believed it could be. I am not saying that everyone who carries sustained pressure will end up standing on a beach watching their daughter leave the country. My situation is my situation and yours will look different. I did not see this coming, and I was not a careless person or an unaware one, and it still reached me, and I could not prevent it because I left it too long. That is all. I wanted to say it plainly because no one said it to me.

Two Strong Houses

After everything that had happened I had to make a phone call that I was dreading, and it was not to a friend or a counsellor or anyone whose job it was to listen. It was to my son's mother. I needed to tell her what was unfolding so she could support him through it on her side, because he was about to move between two homes where the ground had shifted underneath one, and he needed at least one of those homes to feel steady while the other one figured itself out. I was unsettled and unsure how the coming weeks were going to look, and I picked up the phone knowing that the conversation could go in any number of directions depending on how much of the past she wanted to bring into it.

She was calm and firm and kind, and she did not reopen anything that did not need reopening, nor was that my intention. She made it clear that she could not be there for me personally in that moment because that fell outside her role, though she could take additional days with our son while everything was shifting so that he had stability on her side while I managed what was ahead. There was no drama in that call and no revisiting of old ground, just two adults focused on the same child, and that conversation set a tone that I did not fully appreciate then. It showed me what cooperation could look like between two people who were no longer together but still shared the most important thing either of them would ever be responsible for.

I stood in the kitchen after that call for a while. I had not made the phone call about us. She had heard what I told her and responded with her son in mind, and that was it. Two people choosing their child over their own discomfort.

I do not take that for granted because I know it does not work that way for everyone. There are families where separation becomes a battleground and children get pulled into the middle of things that have nothing to do with them, and I am grateful that has not been my experience with either of my children's mothers. My son moves between two homes with the kind of ease that only exists when both parents are committed to making it work, and my daughter's mother has encouraged and supported our relationship across the distance, allowing us to stay connected despite being on opposite sides of the world. Neither of those things were owed to me. They were given, and they have made a difference to my children's lives that I will never underestimate.

There is a conversation that comes up whenever separation involves children, and it usually centres on the idea that staying together under one roof is always better for them than splitting into two homes. I understand the intention behind that because stability matters and children thrive when they feel secure. But what I learned through my own experience is that a house can look intact from the outside while the atmosphere inside it is slowly compressing everyone who lives in it. I had lived in two relationships where the structure held but the air inside it had changed, where the pace I was carrying had seeped into how every room felt, and the children in those homes were absorbing that whether anyone named it or not. Staying under one roof would not have lowered my baseline or widened my capacity. It would have preserved the appearance of stability while the compression continued, and everyone in it would have kept paying the cost.

What I found, and what I was not expecting to find, was that two separate homes functioning with genuine composure gave my children something that one strained home had not been able to give them, two environments where the adults were focused on showing up well for them instead of managing the tension between each other, and they could feel the difference even if they could not have described it. Children do not measure safety by whether their parents share an address. They measure it by how it feels to be in the room with you, by whether your presence settles them or puts them on edge, and two homes where the adults are regulated will always offer a child more safety than one home where the adults are braced.

My son adjusted faster than I expected. The first few weeks he would ask questions at handover, small logistical things about where his bag was or what was happening tomorrow, and I could hear him mapping the new routine in his head. Within a month he had stopped asking. He knew which house had which things and which nights were mine and which were his mother's. He would arrive at the door with his school bag already packed for the next morning and walk in like he had always lived this way. I watched him do that and felt two things at once, pride that he was handling it and sadness that he had to.

That is not me justifying the breakups or pretending that separation was painless or claiming that I have figured out some better way of doing family. I carry the weight of those endings and I carry responsibility for my part in them. What I am saying is that once the decision had been made, the question became what kind of environment my children would move through, and the answer to that question depended entirely on how the adults chose to show up. The coordination required effort and the cooperation required putting things aside that would have been easier to hold onto. But the result was that my children moved between homes where they were loved and where the adults around them were focused on them, and that is something I will always be proud of, even inside the grief of how we got there.

Part Three

Carry It Better

Rebuilding

Healing did not arrive the way I expected it to, and I had expected it enough times to have a clear picture of what it was supposed to look like. I expected a conversation that unlocked something, a moment of clarity that rearranged the way I understood myself, a change in how I woke up one morning compared to the morning before. What happened was slower, messier, and far less legible than that, and the first sign of it was not that things started improving but that I stopped pretending they were fine, which sounds small until you understand how much energy the pretending had been consuming. I started the journey of talking to professionals, not tidying my situation for the person I was saying them to and not building the version of events that made me look good. Some days that meant sitting in a room and crying in a way that felt humiliating and necessary in equal measure, and the humiliation was itself something to work through. I had spent the better part of two decades being the person who held it together in other people's worst moments, and the idea that I was now the one who needed someone to sit with me while I fell apart ran so hard against the grain of how I understood myself, that it took real work to stop feeling like a personal failing.

The support I got helped me understand something, which was a framework for what had actually been happening inside my body across all those years, and once I had that framework I stopped treating what I was experiencing as evidence that I was broken and started treating it as information about a system that had been carrying far more than it was ever designed to hold without any means of discharging it. Understanding alone did not fix anything immediately and I want to be honest about that because I think people expect it to produce change more quickly than it does. What it changed was the relationship I had with what was happening inside me, and that change, turned out to matter more than anything else that came after it, because everything else was built on it.

There wasn't some kind of divine revaluation in the healing. Nobody handed me a formula and I am glad because I think I would have followed it without feeling any of it and missed the point entirely. What happened instead was that I tried things and kept what worked and let the rest go, because I was too depleted to carry anything that was not actually moving something. Writing became part of it, not in any structured way, just putting thoughts somewhere outside my own head so they stopped looping, and what felt formless and overwhelming on the inside looked different once it was on the page, edged, something with a shape I could look at, something that had stopped turning endlessly inside me. Running steadied something that talking alone could not reach, and lifting gave the tension that lived in my body somewhere deliberate to go, so it stopped pooling in my shoulders and jaw. Sleep stopped being something I negotiated around the edges of everything else and became something I protected, because by then I understood that every night I did not rest properly I was feeding the very elevation I was trying to lower. Sitting in stillness for twenty minutes without reaching for a task or a screen was uncomfortable; a clear signal that the system did not trust stillness, that my mind immediately reached for something to solve or plan, and I had to sit inside that discomfort long enough for the body to register that nothing was actually required of it right now. The discomfort softened slowly across many ordinary mornings. I stopped reading silence as the absence of demand and started feeling it as space my body could be inside, and that change, which sounds unremarkable written down, was remarkable when I felt it happening.

My son seemed to lean into me more during this period. I think he noticed the initial change, the way I moved through the house at a pace that did not suggest urgency, his body followed.

If you are reading this and you are the person who is still managing everything on the outside while something underneath has been running hotter than it should, the person who has told themselves they will address it properly once things settle down, sit with something honestly, because I told myself the same thing and the settling I was waiting for did not come. What came instead was the fracture, and the fracture was what made the waiting finally impossible to keep justifying. You do not need to be at the bottom of something to start. You need to be honest enough with yourself to admit that the pace you are carrying is costing more than you are letting on, and that the people around you are already living with the cost of it even if nobody has said so out loud yet.

What I was working toward through all of it, though I could not have named it clearly from inside the process, was the space that sits between feeling something and what you do with it. A gap that had compressed to almost nothing across the years of running elevated. What I was learning, slowly and imperfectly, was that the gap could be rebuilt, that a deliberate pause, practised enough times that it became something the body could actually locate, would widen that space until there was room to choose, and the choosing repeated often enough, would eventually lower the floor I was starting from and widen the range of what I could hold without it spilling.

My capacity grew when I just slowed down a bit. I had to feel that in my own body before I believed it was true, but feeling it took longer than I wanted it to.

There were nights where my body would betray the quiet of the house before I was even conscious of what was happening. I would hear my own voice first, not words, just a sound that came from somewhere deeper than language, the kind of noise fear makes when it cannot find the right shape to come out of, a child's voice really, raw and unguarded, nothing like the voice I wore through the day. My body would be sitting up before my mind had caught up with it, heart already pounding, adrenaline already moving through me at a speed that belonged to whatever my sleeping mind had been replaying, and for those first few seconds there was no bedroom and no safe house. There was only a scared inner voice in a man's body absolutely certain that something was wrong and that it needed to move. Every sound the house made in the dark became information to be assessed. I would lie there long after the dream had dissolved, listening intently to nothing, my system refusing to believe the evidence in front of it that everything was fine.

For a good five years that was what nights looked like, and I can see now exactly why I was always tired, why the days carried a flatness that came from a system that never fully rested.

I never told anyone about the nightmares until I started talking to professionals. The dreams were different every time and this isn't the space to explore them, but the feeling was the same, something collapsing and me unable to move fast enough. I got good at pretending the next morning. A coffee, a run, a shower, and by the time anyone saw me I was the version they expected.

It embarrassed me then and I am still embarrassed by it now. That sound, waking yourself with your own voice, feels like a private thing that should have stayed private, and there is a particular loneliness in lying in the dark after it has happened, when the house is still and your heart is still hammering and you are the only one who knows what just occurred.

What is different now is not that the nightmares

have stopped, because they have not, they have just become less frequent and less consuming when they arrive. I wake to the same sound sometimes, the same internal voice, the same sitting up before I am fully conscious, but what follows is different. I breathe. I get up and have a glass of water and I walk through the house, because the body needs to confirm it for itself, and I check that my son is sleeping, which I know is a perfectly normal thing for a parent to do in the middle of the night. Then I go back to bed and I sleep. The baseline does not run away from me the way it used to, does not climb and stay climbed for the rest of the night, because I have spent enough time working on where it sits that even at three in the morning, even with my heart still coming down, I can find my way back without a long fight. That is not a small thing. It took years to be able to say it.

The work is ongoing and the floor is lower now, which means there is more range available before I reach the edge of it. I can be in a room and let it be quiet. I can hear something that would once have tightened my chest and feel it move through without it locking in. I can show up for my son with something that is presence, and he can feel the difference, which is the thing that matters most to me now, not the understanding I have built or the work I have done, but the fact that he can feel it. That is what the repetition built. It is also what I have to keep building, because the baseline does not hold low on its own and I know now that the moment I stop paying attention to it, it will begin to climb again, and the climbing is enough that you can miss it if you are not watching. Which is exactly how it happened the first time.

The Arc

The hardest part of this to explain is not the pressure or what it did or even what it cost. The hardest part is that I knew. Not at the end, not in hindsight, but all the way through it, a background awareness that sat underneath everything and never fully went away, the knowledge that the pace was too high and the weight was reaching the people around me while I was still inside the momentum of it. I absorbed it and moved through it anyway, because the thing causing the problem was also the thing I believed was holding everything together, and that is what you tell yourself while the cost keeps running.

Responsibility had been accumulating across my adult life. Anyone who takes things seriously would feel it. A career that demanded everything, a son, a second relationship, a daughter, two households, custody weeks, and I had absorbed each addition and adapted because that's what was required. The internal pace had been running high long enough that I had stopped registering it as a state. It had become a personality, the way a sound that has been in a room long enough stops being something you hear and becomes just the room, and the people in my life were living with the consequences of that in ways I was aware of and carried past.

I did love and it was constant and real across the whole of that period, and I want to say that plainly because it is the truest thing I can say about those years. I loved my children and my partner deeply and I meant every expression of it. What the love could not do was protect those people from what I was carrying into the rooms we shared, because love and capacity are different things. What the people in those rooms needed was more room around the feeling, the softness that should have been available at the end of a hard day, the patience that should not have been running out before the week was half done. If I think about the quality of being settled enough in your own body that the people alongside you can feel it, how that must amplify in the opposite. I could not give them that, and I knew it, and I absorbed it all and moved through it because stopping had no shape I could picture and I was afraid of what would happen to everything I was holding if I tried. It was like I knew I had to get this all out, to slow down, but that fear of the vulnerability that would show, caused me to brace against it. Hindsight is a wonderful thing. I've said it before, and I will say it again. I should have spoken to someone.

The fracture came from all that accumulated weight reaching the edge of what the structure could hold, and when it arrived the cost landed on people who had no part in producing it. My son on the couch, my daughter on the other side of the world, the silence of a house that has reorganised itself around an absence. I carried the burden of those things and I still carry them and carrying them honestly was what finally made it possible to see the whole shape of what had been happening.

I have described the cycle already in its pieces. The baseline rising, the range narrowing, the spill-over reaching everyone near me long before anything broke visibly. In the shortened patience and in the tone that lands differently than intended, the atmosphere that changes in rooms you walk into without anyone being able to say exactly why. The spillover is what eventually fractures what you have been trying to hold together. And then there is the movement in the other direction. The awareness of what the pattern was, the deliberate pause, the daily practice of widening the range back out, the slow building of a capacity that had been running on empty for too long. That is the full shape of it. Knowing that something is wrong and never quite doing enough to change it.

You may know that feeling, the low-level awareness that something in the way you are carrying your life is costing the people you love something they have never asked you to name, the sense of being present in every room and not fully available inside any of them. The exhaustion of carrying that knowledge without acting on it, because acting on it means looking honestly at what the pattern has already cost, and that accounting is very difficult to begin.

I talk to people sometimes who describe their own version of this and I can see the recognition in their faces when they hear it from someone else. The details are different and the jobs are different and the relationships are different, but the shape is the same.

I guess the question is why didn't I stop and slow down? Because stopping would mean looking at the whole of it at once, and the whole of it is too much to look at while I was still inside it.

Lowering the Baseline

None of what follows came from a textbook first. It came from sitting in the wreckage of patterns I could not explain and going looking for what might hold. I read Daniel Goleman's work on emotional intelligence and recognised pieces of myself in every gap he described. I came across Daniel Siegel's concept of the window of tolerance, the range within which a person can function without becoming overwhelmed, and it gave me language for what I had been calling baseline and capacity in my own head for months. The skills I describe here grew out of that reading and out of the work itself, shaped by what sustained pressure had done to me and by what I had to rebuild from the ground up. They are not a framework. They are what I found that lowered my baseline. You may find your own skills, that are specific to you.

Understanding these concepts came later than I would have liked. Every part of it was learned through getting it wrong first. There was no guide for any of it. There was no person standing beside me saying do this next. There was me in a house with my son, trying to become the kind of man who could hold what needed holding and put down what needed putting down, and most days I got the balance wrong and tried again the next morning. The unglamourous side of healing.

Once I understood that the elevated baseline was the common denominator in all of it, I stopped waiting for things to settle and went looking deliberately for what worked. What I found were skills that hold each other up, and the most important of them is self-awareness. To me self-awareness was really difficult to practice. It was being in any situation, describing internally what I was feeling and making sure that feeling was proportionate to the situation. If it wasn't that was ok, I was kind to myself and you can adjust. It just takes practice. It is also being aware of other people's feelings. When I look at my son now I can see if he's holding tension, by the way his body is, by the sound of his voice. For most of my adult life I could not notice what was happening inside me let alone what other people were feeling. Slowing down enough to notice became the first work, and it gave me back the choice I had been missing, the gap between feeling something and deciding what to do with it, which is where capacity is either held or lost.

Empathy came from that. I had been treating it as something you performed when someone else was upset, a set of sympathetic responses you delivered while managing your own reaction underneath. When I started listening to my son or the people I was close to without already planning my response while they were still talking, what happened between us changed and I could feel it before I could explain it. People do not need you to solve what they are feeling. They need to feel that you can hold it alongside them by listening, understanding how they feel, and that is what builds capacity between people.

My son came home from school one afternoon and I could tell something was wrong before he said a word. His shoulders were pulled in and he was quieter than usual. Six months earlier I would have asked what happened, listened for thirty seconds, and offered something practical. That afternoon I sat down next to him and said nothing and let the quiet fill the room until he was ready. When he spoke, it was about something so insignificant but it had affected him. I did not try to fix it. I stayed beside him and let him feel what he was feeling, and when he leaned into me I understood what empathy looked like when you were doing it instead of thinking about it. Sometimes, you don't need a fix, you just need someone to be there to listen to you and make you feel ok.

Regulation is the one skill that I had the most backwards. I had been doing a version of it my whole career, absorbing what each day produced and containing it behind a functional exterior. I know these chapters may feel more literary in tone, but I need to share with you what regulation did for me. When I started journalling, I would write down short-term and long-term goals. Over time, I converted these into my regulation skills. Some of these were non-negotiable for me, but with every repetition of these skills, my body learnt not to brace, and over time, that has most certainly lowered my baseline and widened my capacity. The short-term things stop the damage in the moment, and the long -term things lower the floor so they do not have to work as hard. I built all of this from what my own body told me was working, across a long stretch of noticing and adjusting, and it is what keeps the range wide enough that the people I care for get the version of me that can reach them.

Regulation is the one I keep coming back to. I love that it grounds me. When I feel the elevation rising, when I know I am not thinking clearly and something is sitting heavy before I have even named it, these are the notes I reach for. The answer is usually already there. I wish I had found all this earlier, but I did not, and what I have now is the practice of returning to it, which turns out to be enough.

Exercise happens because it is the morning and the morning is when I either go to the gym or run. A standard that removed itself from negotiation. Discipline was built through this, deciding in advance what you will do regardless and then letting that decision carry you on the days when nothing else does. Over time that consistency is what maintains my capacity. Discipline is what nobody talks about because it is the least interesting to describe, but it is the thing that keeps all the others from falling apart. Motivation comes and goes and I have never been able to rely on it, but on the days it is not there what keeps the practice alive is having already decided what I do regardless. I can't tell you how many times I'm driving to the gym at 530 in the morning, unmotivated and tired. But discipline gets me there, because I know that's what I have to do. And the more I did it, the easier it became. With discipline I keep moving forward. You don't let a bad moment, ruin the rest of the day.

There was a morning, several months into the work, where I woke up and my body had not yet decided what it needed to be ready for. I had been waking up already moving for so long that I had forgotten there was any other way to start a day, and that morning was the first signal I trusted that something in the floor had shifted. Those early gym sessions and runs, that discipline, forced a motivation that morning. I wanted to go for a run. I just wanted to run. Not in an urgent way like I had somewhere to be, but a calming calling. It was raining and cold. But I ran, and I didn't stop. It was the raindrops on my face and the comfort that gave me. The bilateral movement that just calmed me. It was addictive. I wasn't out of breath, just at a pace where I could feel the ground beneath me.

I got home that morning and stood in the kitchen and drank a glass of water and my hands were shaking. Not from the cold and not from the running. Something in my body had come loose out there on the path and it had not settled back into place yet. I sat down at the table and put my hands flat on the surface and held them there until the shaking stopped. I carried that feeling with me all day like a stone in my pocket, turning it over, trying to understand what it meant.

Running gave me something I had not found in any conversation or any book. It was not the distance or the time. It was the fact that my body was doing something hard and my mind had no choice but to follow it, and while that was happening the noise in my head went quiet. Not silent. Quiet. Like a room where someone has turned the music down low enough that you can hear yourself think.

Lowering my baseline came in small physical details across ordinary mornings and ordinary evenings. Just like that day. The running is what moved it first and most noticeably. I had been running across the whole of that period as part of managing life, but the running I was doing now was different in intention, and the body knew the difference. It was not burning something off so I could get through the day. It was teaching my system something about what the body could do with accumulated tension, that it could be expended physically and purposefully. The movement would be real, the tension discharged. Lifting weights also did something similar, giving me the stored weight somewhere to land, and the tiredness that came from training hard felt clean. There was no bracing, and my body started to learn the difference between the two.

Sleep was the one that required the most deliberate protection because it was the easiest to negotiate away and the most consequential when I did. Every late night fed the elevation directly, and once I understood that clearly enough I stopped treating sleep as something to be fitted around everything else. The twenty minutes of stillness I started sitting in each morning was uncomfortable at first, my mind going immediately toward whatever was unresolved, and I sat in it anyway because the discomfort was information, a clear signal that still felt dangerous. The only way through that was to keep sitting inside it until the body understood that nothing bad happened inside. Journalling got the looping thoughts out of my head and onto a page, and that alone broke something I had not realised was running. Not deciding to respond to every demand immediately took some of the constant vigilance out of my system that had been burning there across the whole compressed period. And this is where I started writing this book.

A wider range means the same responsibilities and the same pressures but with more room in the body, more room in how I respond, more room for the people around me to feel the difference. That is the whole thing. All those difficult days, stacked up, the discipline, and the movement forward, really lowered my baseline.

There was something else that made the lowering possible, and I want to name it properly because I have not given it the weight it deserves. My son's mother had every reason to make the overseas trips difficult. She did not. When I needed to get on a plane to see my daughter, she adjusted. She covered what needed covering, rearranged what needed rearranging, and did it without requiring negotiation or gratitude. That kind of accommodation is not a small thing when the relationship that produced it has its own fractures, and when the coordination of shared parenting asks of two people who are no longer building a life in the same direction. She gave me the space to be a father to both of my children, even when that meant absorbing the disruption herself, and I am aware that not everyone in her position would have done that. The lowering of my baseline depended on things I could practice and things I could study and things I could sit with, but it also depended on people around me behaving with more generosity than circumstances required of them. She was one of those people, and that generosity gave me room I needed and did not always deserve.

My parents showed up through that period in ways I have not given enough credit to elsewhere in this book. My mother would call and I could hear she had been thinking about me. She would ask how I was and I would say fine and she would pause, and the pause said she knew I was not, and she would let it sit there until I either said something real or changed the subject. My father was quieter. He would turn up and help with things around the house, practical things that did not require talking about feelings, and the steadiness of him being there was its own kind of support. He cooked me food, fixed things around the house, put his tools in the car, and stayed for a cup of tea. He came back the next week without being asked. I was fortunate to have support and generosity from all angles. That's not to say the process was easy. It was incredibly lonely. It was the loneliness of being in a room full of people who care for you and still feeling like there is a pane of glass between you and the rest of the world. People could see me, and I could see them, but I could not always find the words to reach across. In a way I'm glad it was a lonely journey. Sometimes these things need to be done by oneself.

Part Four

Life

When It Returns

Grief still catches up with me sometimes and I do not mind when it does, because it reminds me how much I love her. I can be moving through an ordinary day and something small cuts through, a child somewhere nearby calling out for her dad, and my head turns before I have decided to turn it, my throat closes, and for a moment she is just gone; the body knows it before the mind does. Then it passes and I keep going. I have stopped fighting that, because those moments are the same thing as loving her and I would not want to be without them. I know I'm not the only one carrying grief.

When he talks about her I can see the memory in his face. His eyes go somewhere I cannot follow, back to a living room floor where a baby girl is pulling herself toward him, and he is holding still so she can reach him. He carries those memories the way I carry mine, as physical things. The press of a small hand on his arm. The sound of her laughing when she finally made it to him.

One afternoon he found a drawing she had done. She was too young for it to look like anything but he knew what it was because he had been there when she did it. He held it with both hands and stared at it and then he folded it carefully and put it in his pocket and went back to what he was doing. I watched him do that and I did not say a word. He carried that piece of paper around for a week before it disappeared into a drawer somewhere.

Grief does not follow a schedule. There are weeks where nothing surfaces and the distance becomes something I carry alongside everything else without noticing the weight of it, and then something ordinary arrives and undoes all of that in a few seconds. This is not a sign that something has gone wrong or that the work has stopped holding. It is just what grief does when the love underneath it is still real.

What I used to do was make those moments heavier than they needed to be, because every time the wave came I would immediately turn it into evidence, asking myself whether I should be past this by now, whether I had done enough, whether the fact that it could still land this hard meant something was broken in me, and that second layer of questioning sat on top of the grief and made it harder to move, because the grief moves through on its own when you leave it alone and the questioning pins it in place.

You will have your own version of this, something that lives close enough to the surface that ordinary moments can reach it without warning, and it does not have to be grief, it can be anything that your body has held onto long enough to respond to before you have thought about it. It could be the moment in a meeting where something shifts and you feel it in your chest before you have identified what it is, the message that arrives and lands in your body before you have finished reading it, the particular silence that tells you something is wrong before anyone has said anything. What all those moments have in common is a body that learned to move quickly because that was what kept everything from falling apart, and the floor being lower does not mean those moments stop coming, it means there is enough room around them when they do.

The sadness rises, and I remain steady within it, not pushing it away or amplifying it, allowing it to move at its own pace until it recedes into the background again. Nothing breaks apart when it happens, and nothing needs to be rebuilt afterwards. The moments that catch me most are not the ones I anticipate. Her birthday I know is coming. Christmas morning, I have thought about it for weeks before it arrives. I have given myself room for those and they land the way difficult things land when you have made space for them, fully but without knocking everything else over. It is the random Wednesday that undoes the preparation. I was in the car a few months ago, nothing significant happening, a song came on that she would have danced to, one of those ridiculous ones she had heard somewhere and decided was her favourite for about three weeks, and my chest closed before I had registered what was happening. I sat in the car park for a few minutes. Then it passed and I drove home. What is different now is that it passes. The wave moves through and the structure around it holds, and I get back in the car and go. That is the whole change.

He does it out of nowhere too. There is no song, no photo, no obvious trigger, just an ordinary moment and then he looks at me and says it. Dad,

I miss her. Not thrown away, not casual, but in the way someone says something they have been sitting on for a while, like he had been building up to it and finally decided today was the day. And every time he does it I feel two things at once, the grief of it for him and the weight of knowing he has been carrying that on his own, tucking it away somewhere inside himself because that is just how he is built. He is so resilient that you would never see it unless he decided to show you, and when he decides to show you it lands.

Then he goes further. He does not just say he misses her in the general sense. He gets specific. I miss her crawling on me. And that detail undoes me every time because I know exactly what he means and I know why it matters so much to him. His strongest memories of her are from when she was between zero and one, when she was just mobile enough to pull herself across the floor and find him wherever he was and climb on him and bother him the way little sisters bother older brothers, and he would pretend to be annoyed while clearly loving every second of the attention. That is what lives in him when he thinks of her. Not the distance or the complexity of what happened, just a small person who used to crawl on him on an ordinary morning when the house was still and nobody had anywhere to be.

I am not the main story in those moments. I know that and I sit with it. This whole book carries the carry it better theme, and yes it is my story, but when my son looks at me and says something like that, I feel for him in a way that goes beyond what I can write cleanly on a page. He is doing his own version of carrying it, at an age where he should not have to, and he does it with such a grace that I am still catching up to.

The Stranger

The thought arrived one morning when I met a friend for coffee and we were sitting down enjoying the sun by the ocean. We had been talking about relationships in general but with everything that had happened I had not fully grasped what I was about to feel. What happens when we both move on? What would that look like? Was it the idea of her with someone else?, which burned more than I wanted to admit. Was it what that meant for my daughter?, someone new coming into her daily life, becoming the presence, I was not. I guess those questions arise for anyone past a relationship, and I know it was just part of the process. I did a lot of journalling trying to get underneath it, and what I kept arriving at was something harder to sit with than jealousy. It was the feeling of being punished for doing the right thing. Ironically I had been self-aware enough in the worst moments to let her go, to put my daughter's stability above my own need to be close, and now that kindness had a cost I had not seen when I made the decision. Someone else would be there for the ordinary evenings. Someone else would be the consistent presence in my daughter's life that I had given up the right to be. I had made a choice out of love and I was going to carry the consequences of it for the rest of my life, and some days that felt less like wisdom and more like a life sentence I had written for myself.

The writing I did through that period was some of the hardest I have put down. I kept arriving at the same question from different angles, trying to find a version of the answer that did not cost me anything, and every time I wrote it out the answer was the same. I had done what I believed was right for her, and the cost of that decision was mine to carry. There was no version of events where I got to keep my daughter close and also give her the stability I believed she needed. Writing that out over and over did not make it hurt less but it made the edges clearer, and clarity, even painful clarity, is easier to carry than something you have not looked at properly.

But I could not live inside that story forever. The punishment narrative is a comfortable place to sit because it makes you the person who did everything right and still got hurt, and there is a kind of identity in that which is easy to hold onto. The truth is more ordinary than that. People move on. That is what happens after relationships end, and it happens at its own pace regardless of how much either person is still processing.

What I had not expected was how physical it felt. There would be a drop in my stomach that arrived before I had even finished the thought, a tightening across my chest that had nothing to do with what was in front of me, a heat that moved through and was gone before I could name it. I wanted to read all of that as evidence of something unresolved, something that still needed fixing, but the more I sat with it the more I understood it was just my body registering an absence it had grown used to.

The hardest part was the comparison, and I do not think I am alone in that. I would catch myself measuring how I was doing against how she appeared to be doing, reading her visible movement as some kind of commentary on where I was, as though her pace said something about mine. It took a while to see that for what it was, because what is visible from the outside has almost nothing to do with what is happening inside someone, and two people processing the end of the same thing will always do it differently and neither way is a verdict on the other.

There were certain songs, certain times of day, certain things that would surface without warning and carry more weight than I expected, not enough to knock everything over, just enough to remind me something real had existed. I stopped trying to make that feeling mean something beyond what it was. It was just recognition, the body acknowledging what had been there, and I could let it pass without turning it into a case for or against anything.

Saturday mornings were one of those. I would be in the kitchen making breakfast for my son and something would come on the radio and I would be somewhere else entirely, standing in a different kitchen in a different country with a baby on my hip and the smell of coffee and the sound of traffic outside the window. My son would say something and I would come back and he would be looking at me the way children look at you when they know you have gone somewhere they cannot follow, and I would smile and ask him what he said and carry on.

What I had to let go of was the need for it to have a particular shape on her end. I was not looking for her to struggle, and I was not looking for signs that it had cost her something, but I noticed there was a part of me that wanted some kind of confirmation that what we had mattered, as though her moving forward at her own pace was somehow evidence that it had not. That is ego, and it is worth naming it plainly. I was not central to her daily life anymore, and that required an adjustment that had nothing to do with how much or how little any of it had meant.

What we had was real. It does not need her to stay still for that to remain true, and it does not need me to carry the weight of it forever to honour it. She can move forward and so can I, and neither of those things cancels what existed. The ache in that is real too, and I am not pretending it is not there, but it sits differently now, more like something I carry than something that carries me, and that is about as much as you can ask of it.

If you have been here, you know how it feels. You did the right thing, the awkward thing, the thing that cost you the most, and somehow that is the thing for which you are still paying. That is one of the cruelest parts of this entire process and I do not think enough people say it aloud. Doing the right thing does not protect you from the aftermath. It just means you carry the aftermath knowing you made the best call you could, and some days that is enough and some days it is not, and both of those are fine.

You're Here

Distance does not remove love. It stretched it, and I felt that stretch physically the first time I stood in the arrivals hall after I had just landed, knowing she was somewhere at the other end of that space, moving toward me. I had just come off a long flight, my body steady in the way it becomes after hours of sitting still, yet underneath that steadiness there was something tighter, something held, below panic, below restlessness, sitting right beneath the surface where I could not put it down. The terminal was bright and loud and none of it reached me. I was not searching for her in the way people scan crowds for someone arriving. I knew she was already there, moving closer, and my body knew it before my eyes confirmed it. I heard her before I saw her.

"Daddy!"

The sound cut through everything. People were still walking past, luggage wheels still rolling across the floor, announcements still echoing overhead, and none of it registered because she was already running toward me. There was no hesitation in her movement, no pause to orient herself, just a direct line that carried everything she felt. My body responded before thought had time to organise itself, stepping forward to meet her without deciding to. When she hit my chest, the force of it was both familiar and intensified by the time apart, and something in me unlocked that I had not realised I was holding.

I wrapped my arms around her and felt her settle into me, the way she always had, as though that space had remained available without interruption, and I noticed her breathing slow against me, bringing mine down with it. There was no rush to move, no need to break the moment to match the pace of the surrounding environment, and we stayed there longer than most people would in a space designed for movement rather than stillness. I remember hearing someone nearby react to what they were seeing, a small acknowledgement that the moment had reached beyond just us, yet it did not change how it felt from inside. It was not something performed or heightened. It was direct. It was human. It was exactly what it needed to be, without adding anything.

That embrace was not the relief I had expected. It did not feel like something that had been missing had suddenly been restored. It felt like confirmation. It showed me plainly that nothing essential had been reduced by the time apart, and that what existed between us had held its structure without needing constant proximity to sustain it. Distance had not thinned anything or worn it down at the edges. It had clarified it by removing the noise of everyday familiarity, leaving only what held without it. I could feel that clarity in the way my body responded, in the way hers did, in the way the moment settled without strain.

The visits that followed took on a deliberate shape, structured around school terms and time zones instead of convenience or impulse. In the first eighteen months, I travelled more than I would have considered sustainable under any other circumstances. Six trips across the world in 18 months, each one carrying a different kind of weight to the travel I had known before, because there was no novelty attached to it, no sense of escape or variation. There were no drinks at departure lounges, no anticipation of something new waiting at the other end, just a clear calculation of time, with each day with her measured and held, aware of how quickly it would pass. The flights became spaces where there was nothing to manage and nothing to distract from the reality of what I was doing, suspended above everything with time to think, unavoidable rather than optional.

Each trip carried a split that remained consistent even as everything else settled into rhythm, with anticipation and the weight of leaving my son behind sitting together on the way there, and a heaviness accompanying the return as I stepped back into routine without her. The plane became a place where that split was most visible, where there was no external structure to contain it, just hours where reflection moved through without interruption. I noticed that I did not try to escape that space the way I might have before; instead, I let it unfold, holding both sides of what I was doing without trying to resolve them into something simpler.

When we were together, time did not feel rushed, yet it carried a density that made each day feel fuller than its length suggested, as though the awareness of its limits sharpened everything inside it. We moved through simple things without elevating them, spending time in parks, taking small holidays, walking hand in hand through places that belonged to neither of our countries and felt shared regardless of geography. There were moments where she would look up at me and say something simple that carried more than anything extended. "You're here!"

There was no accusation in it, no reference to the time apart, no indication that she was measuring what had been missed. It was just a statement of presence, acknowledged without drama, and those moments held more stability than anything that tried to explain or compensate for distance.

She said it differently every time. Sometimes as a greeting and sometimes in the middle of an ordinary moment when she would look up from whatever she was doing and see me and say it like she was confirming something she already knew. There was no performance in it, just a child telling her father she could see him. I have replayed those moments more times than I can count.

I have seen what happens when separated parents let their own positions sit between them and the child. I have watched it from close enough to know what it costs. That has not been our story, and I am aware of why. The support from the mothers of my children has allowed that to hold, and I do not overlook it, because I know it is not guaranteed. Every arrival that felt easy, every handover that carried no tension, every phone call where she sounded settled and happy on the other end, those things did not happen by accident. They happened because the people around her made room for me to stay present, and because I did not give them a reason to stop.

Distance works because the structure around it works, and because her life where she remains stable in ways that do not require my presence to maintain. She has a routine, school, friends, and a rhythm that is hers, and I respect that rhythm rather than trying to reshape it to fit my own preferences. The communication between her mother and me stays practical and clear, focused on what she needs rather than what either of us might want to assert, and that consistency has removed the kind of friction that would otherwise distort what sits between our children and us. I am aware that not every father has that experience, and that awareness stays with me, keeping me grounded in my approach.

The airport became a rhythm over time, something I moved through repeatedly, and it still carried weight but it no longer knocked me off balance. Anticipation, the moment of impact, time that felt both full and limited, the goodbye, the return. The early departures carried a heaviness that felt difficult to contain, sitting on the plane with everything present at once. Yet, gradually something shifted, not in the love itself but in my capacity to hold it without losing balance. I could say goodbye and feel it fully and still stand up. I could return home and remain steady. I could carry both parts of my life at the same time.

Part Five

Capacity

The Floor

I lived with the sense that something in me was slightly off, sitting just beneath the surface of how I moved through the day, shaping the tone of my reactions without fully declaring itself. I could feel it in the pace I carried, in the slight elevation that stayed present even in ordinary moments, in the way insignificant things sometimes landed with more edge than they needed to. I was aware of it, though I could not fully name it. Instead of lowering it, I learned how to adjust around it, structuring my responses, my routines, even my interactions to compensate for that underlying tension without addressing it directly. It became a background condition that I managed but never resolved, something I worked with but never questioned, and over time, that approach felt normal enough that I stopped expecting anything different.

What changed over those years unfolded through repetition and awareness rather than intention. I became slower in ways that were not visible on the outside, less immediate in my reactions, more willing to stay inside a feeling and let it be there, and more conscious of the atmosphere I was creating, without defending it when it became uncomfortable. Not every internal movement required an external response, and that space was something I had not had before. The shift was subtle enough that it did not feel like progress while it was happening, yet over time it changed the way I experienced situations that once would have pulled me into a tighter, more reactive state.

The loss of my daughter remained. The distance remained regardless of how I changed. The regret still surfaced at times, often without warning, and the awareness of what had shifted in our lives remained present without being revisited consciously. What changed was not the presence of those feelings, but the way they moved through everything else, because they no longer spread into areas that did not belong to them. They could exist and not take over. They did not shape every interaction or colour the tone of the entire day the way they used to.

I noticed it in ordinary moments, in the way situations that once would have escalated remained contained, in the way a room could hold steady even when emotion entered it. There was a growing capacity to stay present without bracing against what I was feeling. A conversation that would once have sharpened would stay level, and I would notice later that it had, without having tried to make it so. That is what capacity felt like in practice: not an absence of emotion but room around it, enough to feel something without it immediately becoming something I said or did.

There was a moment that made that clearer to me than anything I had previously understood, and it did not arrive in a setting that felt significant, but in a small, ordinary space that held more than I expected.

My son was seven, and he had been crying after getting in trouble over something minor, the kind of situation that would usually pass quickly and return to normal without leaving anything behind. That afternoon felt different; I could not immediately explain why, the house carried a louder tone than usual, and his crying stayed with me and did not settle the way it normally would. I could feel it in my chest as something that lingered rather than moved on, and I noticed that I was carrying more than just that moment without fully recognising what else was present.

I walked into the bathroom and sat on the floor, not with a clear intention, but with a sense that I needed a moment to collect myself before returning to the situation. As I sat there, the surface layer of what I was feeling began to shift. I hated seeing him upset, and that feeling opened something beyond the immediate situation, because beneath it lay everything that had been accumulating over the previous years. The distance from my daughter, the grief that had not fully resolved, the weight of what had changed in our lives, all of it surfaced at once, sudden, even though it had been sitting there underneath everything. It was as though the moment created enough space for everything else to come forward, and I found myself sitting there with an awareness that was larger than the room I was in. I could not breathe. My eyes were filling, and I was trying so hard not to make a sound. I thought I was alone in that moment, and I allowed myself to sit inside it without trying to move away from it.

But I was not alone. My son stood in the doorway, his face still marked by his own crying, and when he saw me sitting there, something in him shifted from what he had been feeling into something more observant. Even at seven, he understood more than I had given him credit for. He was aware of his sister's absence in a way that had shaped him as well. But inside all that, he still walked over slowly, without urgency, and said in a steady voice that did not carry hesitation, "Just breathe, Dad. It will be okay," as he put his arms around me. Simple and direct. His arms were small enough that they could not reach all the way around me and I could feel his hands pressing flat against my back, and his breathing was steady against my side, slow and deliberate, and I matched it without thinking. My breath found his rhythm and in that small room on that bathroom floor my seven-year-old was doing for me what I had spent months learning how to do for myself.

Something in me opened in that small room.

Nothing on the outside had changed and nothing had been fixed. It was still enough to stay with what I was feeling and not move away from it. We stayed there together for a while, breathing, and neither of us were trying to fix anything, letting the moment be what it was. At some point we laughed, a small laugh that did not erase what had been felt but sat alongside it.

That moment changed something in how I understood stillness, because I had been associating it with weakness, with an absence of direction, and I began to see that it required something harder than action to remain present without reacting. It took me years to learn what he was already demonstrating in that moment, that steadiness, that allowed emotion to exist without turning it into something that needed to be managed immediately. He had absorbed, through his own experience, a way of being that I had taken decades to arrive at and seeing that in him showed me what it meant to create safety.

What creates safety is the ability to stay present with emotion without letting it disrupt the environment. My son did not need me to appear unaffected to feel secure. He needed consistency in presence, a sense that emotion could exist without becoming something he had to carry alone.

In the years between those moments, I watched him grow in ways that reflected that same pattern of learning through repetition, and I saw in him both the difficulty and the willingness to move through it. I have seen frustration rise in him in ways that felt familiar, and I have seen him overwhelmed in moments when the response could easily have escalated. Yet, I have also seen him pause, reset, and try again without being guided through every step. None of that happened automatically, and it did not arrive without effort. It was built through small repetitions that accumulated over time, shaping how he responded to what he felt.

That afternoon in the bathroom, I did not want my grief to spill into him and make it something he had to carry, and I was conscious of the line between allowing emotion to exist and allowing it to become something that affected him directly. Yet when he came in and sat beside me, he showed me something that changed my understanding in a humbling way, because he did not need me to remove that part of myself to feel safe. He met me in that space without hesitation, and in doing so, he changed the dynamic from something I felt responsible for containing to something we could sit within together without it becoming overwhelming.

Two years earlier, I would have approached that moment with a different posture, feeling the need to absorb everything for him, to prevent any part of my internal state from becoming visible in a way that might affect him. On that floor, something had changed without me realising it fully. We were both sitting with the same thing, and that was different. The loss had not disappeared, the distance had not changed, and the past remained exactly as it was.

The pain of everything was still there, unchanged in its presence and in what it represented, and it had not been reduced or removed through time or understanding. What had changed was the way we held it, the way it moved through the space between us without creating tension or resistance that needed managing. We were no longer bracing against it as we once had. That absence of bracing created a steadiness that did not rely on removing what was difficult but on allowing it to exist without shaping everything around it. The weight was still there. We were just no longer bracing against it.

Capacity is Practice

I have been telling myself that some people are just wired calmer, because that explanation let me off the hook. If reactivity was built in, there was nothing to examine and nothing to change. It took me a while to see what was actually happening. The pace I carried was not personality. It was what I had practised most consistently, years of urgency run through my body over and over until it was the only setting I had.

I had practised being reactive for over a decade. Every time I responded before I had fully registered what I was feeling, every time I let the pace override the pause, I was teaching my body that speed was the answer to discomfort, and my body learned that lesson so well it became the only lesson it knew.

Lowering the baseline of tension creates more available space. I could create moments when things appeared calm on the surface, when my voice remained even, and my behaviour stayed composed. I interpreted that as progress without recognising what was happening underneath. Discomfort still carried urgency, and even when it was not visible externally, it was pressing internally for some form of release, looking for a way to move through tone, correction, or withdrawal. As capacity increased, that urgency began to soften, and the discomfort did not disappear but it stopped demanding to be dealt with immediately. It could exist in the body without converting into behaviour. That shift altered not only how I experienced those moments, but how others experienced me within them, because the atmosphere of a room changes when intensity is held rather than discharged.

There was a period when composure itself was enough. If nothing appeared out of place on the outside, I counted that as progress. But I was tight without showing it, held together through constant adjustment, and the effort required to stay that way was its own kind of strain. The emotion had not moved anywhere. It had been compressed into a smaller space, and I was spending energy keeping it there. That is suppression, and it looks like steadiness until it surfaces somewhere else. When I finally felt capacity, I did not have to hold anything down. Emotion passed through and the body stayed where it was.

The changes did not feel like changes while they were happening. They came through ordinary moments that passed without acknowledgment. I would feel irritation and not sharpen my language. I would sit with sadness and not withdraw from the room. I would notice something rising in my chest during a conversation and let it stay there instead of letting it move into my voice. None of those moments felt significant on their own, and there was no clear point where everything shifted. Yet over time, the threshold moved, noticeable in retrospect, because situations that once created urgency no longer carry the same pull.

Nobody sees this work happening. There is no acknowledgement for choosing to pause before responding, for softening a reaction that would have previously been sharper. What changes is what does not happen. Tension stays where it is instead of being passed on. A room holds steady instead of shifting.

I remember a day when my son was overtired and everything was too much for him. He could not find his school shirt and he was crying and saying he was going to be late and I could feel the old reaction building in me, the urge to fix it quickly, to tell him it was fine, to find the shirt and hand it to him and move on. Instead, I got down to his level and put my hand on his back and waited. He cried for another minute and then he took a breath and looked at me and said he was alright. I asked if he wanted help looking and he said yes and we found it together, under his bed where it had fallen. The whole thing took three minutes. Six months earlier it would have taken three minutes too but it would have ended differently. I would have found the shirt, handed it to him, told him to hurry up, and he would have gone to school carrying my impatience alongside his own frustration.

You might recognise this in your own experience. The voice stays level, the response comes out measured, and from the outside nothing appears wrong. But if you are someone who has been carrying a lot, you know the difference between what that looks like and what it costs. The work is not visible because it is internal. You can sit with something that wants to move outward, choose not to pass it on, and nobody around you will know that happened. Those moments add up, and that is where capacity shifts. Not in the conversation you handled well because you were feeling fine, but in the one you held steady when you were not.

I could see the patterns clearly and still find myself moving through them the same way when the conditions were present. Knowing what was happening did not change how my body responded when it happened. I could name the compression and still feel it tighten. I could recognise the elevation and still watch myself react from inside it. What changed me was not the understanding but the repetition, staying inside uncomfortable moments without converting them into action, and doing that enough times that my body stopped bracing the way it used to. That is slower work than I expected, and there is no shortcut through it.

The body remembers both ways of being. It remembers the speed and it remembers the stillness, and on difficult days the speed comes back.

The difference now is that I can feel it happening and I can choose to let it pass. That choice gets easier with practice but it never becomes automatic. I do not think it is supposed to.

As that tolerance grew, the way I read situations began to change. I stopped reading silence as rejection, and a delay in someone's response no longer felt like instability. Emotion is still present and felt fully, yet it is not intensified by the urgency that once surrounded it, which creates more space around each experience. Within that space, proportion becomes clearer, and what is happening can remain contained within its actual context rather than expanding into something larger. A comment remains a comment without becoming evidence of something broader, and a moment of frustration remains specific rather than turning into a narrative that extends beyond the situation itself.

The difference lies in the relationship to immediacy, in the way the reflex to convert sensation into action softens, allowing a gap to exist between what is felt and what is done. Within that gap, there is room to remain present without being pulled into reaction, and that room creates a form of steadiness that is not dependent on external conditions. The feelings continue to rise, grief still moves when it surfaces, disappointment still lands when expectations are not met, yet they no longer dictate the direction of behaviour in the way they once did.

The way that weight moves through me has formed into something that feels less restrictive. It no longer presses everything around it, and it does not move outward into spaces that did not create it in the same way it once did. More can be held without it becoming something that needs to be shared prematurely. The change has influenced how I experience pressure, and how others experience me within it.

The thing with capacity is that it is not fixed. It is not something you are born with a set amount of and have to ration for the rest of your life. You can widen it. You can stretch it. You can build it, slowly and gently, at any point you choose. And I think that is one of the most important things I have learned, because for so long I believed my limits were simply who I was. They were not. They were just the edges of a container I had never thought to expand.

So, if there is anything I want you to take from this, it is that you do not have to wait. You do not have to hit the wall I hit. You do not have to lose something, or someone, to finally give yourself permission to grow. You can begin now, softly, in the middle of an ordinary week, without a crisis forcing your hand. Just please, do not wait for loss the way I did.

Depth Over Intensity

Intensity, to me, once felt like proof: anything that registered sharply in my body carried a sense of certainty that I did not question. If something cut through quickly, it mattered. If a reaction rose fast and strong, it felt honest. If love arrived with force, if it pulled attention inward and filled the space with urgency, I interpreted that as depth rather than asking what was driving it. I moved through relationships and responsibility, holding that assumption in place, believing the force of a feeling was a reliable indicator of its meaning.

Looking back, I can see how often what I labelled as depth was a system running hot, a state where urgency created a sense of aliveness that felt convincing enough to trust without further reflection.

Intensity can resemble passion at first, because both carry energy and both create movement, yet intensity often comes from compression rather than clarity. It builds pressure quickly and looks for release just as quickly, pushing for answers before understanding has had time to form, escalating small misunderstandings into something that feels more significant than it is. I noticed how easily friction could feel like instability, how quickly I would move to resolve or correct it rather than allowing space for things to settle, and how often emotional volume was mistaken for emotional truth. When your baseline is elevated, and capacity is limited, intensity becomes the most available register, and it dominates through immediacy. It creates spikes that feel meaningful in the moment, yet those spikes do not sustain themselves, and what follows is often a drop that leaves behind fatigue rather than clarity.

Depth moves differently, and it took me time to recognise that difference. It does not announce itself the way intensity does, and it does not rely on heightened states to validate itself. It allows feeling to exist without amplifying it, and it creates space for connection. Attraction can be there and not turn into possession, and care can exist and not try to direct or manage the other person. That pace felt unfamiliar at first, because I had not lived there consistently. Without the markers of intensity, it was easy to misinterpret steadiness as a lack of depth rather than a different form of it. Over time, I noticed that what felt less dramatic was also more stable, and that stability allowed connection to develop without being disrupted by the need for constant reinforcement.

I felt it on an ordinary evening. I was on a park bench reading something and my son was drawing in the sand, and neither of us were talking.

The sun was still up and it was summer but the park was quiet and there was no urgency in what we were doing. I looked down at him and he was concentrating, his tongue between his teeth the way it goes when he is focused, and I felt something I had not felt before, a fullness that did not need anything else added to it.

What I understand now is how to engage with love without measuring its value by intensity. I am no longer drawn to volatility framed as chemistry because I can recognise the pattern of elevation that lies beneath it, and I am less interested in experiences that require constant proof of their significance through emotional force. My attention has shifted toward steadiness, toward conversations that can move at a natural pace without pressure, toward friction that does not threaten the foundation of what exists. That kind of connection does not depend on intensity to feel real, and it does not require escalation to maintain itself, yet it asks for a different level of presence, one that is less reactive and more grounded.

Openness, within that shift, has taken on a different meaning for me, because it is no longer tied to expression alone or to the idea of sharing everything without filter. It is not needing the armour anymore. It is saying what is true and not bracing for what comes back. It is seeing what is there and not trying to make it look better than it is. I have learned to recognise how easily fear can present itself as anger, how quickly uncertainty can turn into grasping, and how often protection can become distance when it is not examined. Containment without openness creates isolation. It keeps everything internal, preventing connections from forming around it; openness without containment can be overwhelming because it lacks the structure needed to hold what is being expressed. The balance between the two is where depth begins to stabilise, allowing emotion to move without distorting the space it exists within.

Choosing depth does not mean reducing feeling

or becoming restrained. What it changes is the relationship to that emotion because it removes the need for it to prove itself through urgency or disruption. I have found that when I am regulated enough to stay present, love no longer needs instability to feel meaningful, and another person's emotion can exist alongside mine without creating a shift that pulls me out of my own centre. There is less need to interpret, less need to resolve immediately, and less pressure to define something before it has had time to take shape. Connection can unfold without being directed by uncertainty, allowing it to settle into something that feels grounded rather than reactive.

For the first time, I feel ready to make a connection from that place. I am less braced and less inclined to move quickly toward certainty. I have patience now that was not there before. What once felt like depth reveals itself as elevation when I look at it closely. I no longer need urgency to feel connected.

My life was intense without knowing it had another side. Urgency felt like passion, relief felt like love, and the adrenaline of something intense felt like proof that it mattered. I had no reference point for the other state because I had never regulated enough to live inside it. Depth felt like absence to me, like something was missing, because it did not announce itself the way intensity did. I know the difference now in my body, not just in my understanding, and that difference is what I am carrying into whatever comes next.

Part Six
Steady

Carrying Without Bracing

There is a difference between being strong and being tight, and I did not recognise how closely I was living to that line, because the way I carried responsibility made both feel like the same thing in practice. I carried responsibility as if it required constant engagement, as if stepping back even slightly would leave something unattended that should have been managed. That posture followed me into situations that did not demand it. My body stayed slightly prepared even in calm moments, holding readiness that shaped how I moved through the day without me questioning it. I would walk into a room already scanning for what could shift, already positioning myself to respond before anything had happened. I would enter conversations already prepared to correct, reassure, or stabilise without first allowing them to unfold. It felt efficient in the moment because I was rarely caught off guard, capable because I could respond quickly, and adult because it aligned with how I understood responsibility. What I did not recognise was that I was rarely fully at rest, and that this constant state of readiness, while functional, was shaping how much of each moment I could experience.

Bracing is not dramatic in the way it is often imagined, and it does not require visible tension to exist, because it can sit beneath composed behaviour without drawing attention to itself. It is a subtle readiness that never completely softens, a way of holding yourself slightly forward even when nothing is pressing against you. It shows up in solving before listening, in preparing for instability even when the ground is steady. You can function well within it, and you can even succeed, because it creates a responsiveness that appears effective from the outside. Yet it limits something less visible because you do not expand within that posture. There is less room to take things in fully, less space to let moments unfold without interference, and, over time, that narrowing becomes part of how you experience everything.

Carrying without bracing feels different, and the difference is clearer the more it is lived, and it does not require stepping away from responsibility or lowering expectations. The same things still need to be held and responded to. What changes is the relationship to anticipation because there is a growing trust that you can respond when something requires you, rather than living in preparation for what might, and that trust allows a different posture to take shape. It means standing upright without leaning forward into imagined impact, allowing situations to present themselves before deciding how to meet them. Space opens where there was previously constant engagement. In that space, there is more clarity, more steadiness, and less pressure to move before it is necessary, which changes how both responsibility and connection are experienced.

I notice this most clearly in ordinary moments because those are the places where my previous posture used to operate without interruption or question. When my son speaks, I let him finish before shaping the outcome, which allows him to express himself fully without being redirected or managed mid-sentence, creating a different kind of interaction between us. When something goes wrong, I allow the initial surge to move through before deciding what to do, and that pause creates enough distance to respond in a way that reflects the situation rather than the first reaction. When the house is still, I do not automatically fill it, because I no longer interpret stillness as a problem to solve or something that needs to be replaced with activity, and that has begun to feel like part of the structure rather than an absence within it.

Responsibility remains, and the demands have not changed: deadlines still exist, and parenting still requires structure and consistency that cannot be avoided or reduced. What has shifted is how that responsibility is carried: it feels distributed now, allowing movement without compression. It sits on the frame now, not in the chest, and it moves through me instead of pressing against me. The weight is still there and still needs to be carried, yet it no longer shapes every movement the same way or creates the same level of internal pressure.

There is also something relational in this shift that becomes more visible over time, because when you are not braced, you do not enter connection defensively or with an underlying expectation that something needs to be managed. Friction does not read as threat, and uncertainty does not immediately feel like instability. There is more room to let things exist before deciding what they need. You allow space for another person to be imperfect without preparing to manage it. That space changes the tone of everything because it removes the underlying tension of anticipating disruption. That shift does not require effort in the moment, yet it alters how connection unfolds, making it feel more open and less defended.

My parents were carrying something of their own through all of it, and I did not fully see that while I was inside the worst of it. They watched their son struggle with separation, and they sat with the kind of helplessness that comes from parental responsibility and not being able to fix what is in front of them. But there was something else underneath their worry that I understood later, it was harder to name. The separation meant distance from their granddaughter. She was not in the country anymore, which meant she was not coming for Sunday lunch or family events, the kind of ordinary accumulation that grandparents build with grandchildren without knowing they are building it. They had their own loss running alongside mine, and they were carrying it without making it mine to hold. They asked how I was doing. They showed up when I needed help and most importantly, they supported my son when I felt like they could offer him more than I could, and they did it without asking for anything back. I did not say thank you for that enough. I am saying it now, because what they carried during that period was real, and it cost them something, and they carried it anyway without letting it become another weight on top of mine.

Carrying without bracing has made me slower in ways that matter, and that slowing has not reduced my ability to respond but it has changed how I respond. I am slower to judge, slower to escalate, and slower to withdraw. That pace allows more information to become visible before action is taken, which leads to responses that are more proportionate and grounded. It has not made me weak, nor has it reduced what I can handle; yet it has made me steadier and more consistent across different situations.

The old posture required constant vigilance because it was built on the idea that I needed to be prepared for anything at any time and that vigilance kept my system engaged even when it did not need to be. This one requires trusting my own ability to respond when something real happens, without staying braced in anticipation. That trust changes how I move through situations because I am no longer relying on being ready to feel capable; instead, I am relying on my capacity to meet what is in front of me.

The weight has not disappeared, and the responsibility has not lessened in what it asks of me or in how it needs to be carried. I simply no longer hold it with my shoulders raised. In that shift, there is a steadiness that was not available to me before, one that allows me to carry what is mine without shaping everything around the expectation of impact.

I want to speak to you for a moment, not as someone who has figured it all out, but as someone who has lived inside the tension of holding too much for too long. I want you to know that the goal was never to stop carrying. Life will always give you things to carry. People you love, responsibilities that matter, seasons that ask more of you than you feel ready to give. The goal is to learn how to carry without bracing. To hold what is yours to hold without locking every muscle in your body against it. Because bracing is what wears you down. Bracing is what turns a heavy week into a heavy year. The weight itself is rarely what breaks us. It is the way we grip it, the way we tense around it, the way we forget to breathe while we are holding it. So if there is one thing I hope you take from this chapter, it is this. You are allowed to soften while you carry. You are allowed to loosen your shoulders, to set things down for a moment, to let the people around you see the weight instead of hiding it behind a steady face. Carrying without bracing is not weakness. It is the quiet, practiced strength of someone who has finally learned that holding on and holding tight are not the same thing.

The Standard

Everyone has carried something they did not ask for and sat inside a life that looked manageable from the outside and felt like drowning from the inside. If you have seen yourself anywhere in these pages, that is enough. But with that recognition comes accountability.

How differently I operated depending on where I was is what bothered me once I had enough distance to look at it honestly. At work I could walk into a situation that would overwhelm most people and hold the room together with a composure that others relied on. I could process what was happening quickly, make decisions under pressure, and give people around me the feeling that someone was in charge and that things were going to be handled. I was good at it, and it gave me a sense of value that I carried with me. Then I would come home and find myself moving through the evening at the same operational pace, treating a conversation with my partner the way I would treat a briefing, moving it toward resolution before she had finished telling me what she needed me to hear. A question would land and I would already be formulating the fix before I had taken the time to understand what was really being asked. I was efficient in my own home, and it made sense to me and baffled the person living inside it with me.

I am not saying that to assign blame in any direction. I am saying it because it is what happened, and because I think a lot of people living at that pace experience something similar and have no language for what it is. You arrive at the environment that demands performance with everything you have, and the people who need your presence get what is left, and you do not do that on purpose. It happens because your system has been shaped by sustained pressure to prioritise output over connection, and because output is visible and measurable and gets acknowledged, while presence is unmeasurable and only noticed by the people around you when it is missing. I could feel the gap between how I showed up at work and how I arrived home, and the gap between them sat in me without explanation. I just knew it was there, sitting underneath everything, and I did not know what to do with it other than carry it.

I did not lose accountability in one visible moment. It was smaller than that, and the smallness of it was the problem. A shift in tone I did not catch before it landed. A response that arrived a half-second too fast, already shaped by something that had nothing to do with the person in front of me. If you have been on the receiving end of that kind of inconsistency, you know it does not need to be dramatic to land. Your partner feels the shift before it becomes a word. They feel your pace, your tension, the difference between you being in the room and you being present in it, and they carry the weight of that. Intimacy does not smooth over small shifts in behaviour. The closer someone stands to you, the more clearly they feel what is not being said, and what might pass unnoticed elsewhere becomes something that shapes the atmosphere of your home.

Two people cannot build anything together if what one person claims to value falls apart when things get hard. I had to look closely at that in myself. I had to look closely at whether what I claimed to value remained present when conditions were not ideal, because it is easy to hold standards when nothing is testing them. If I say steadiness matters, it cannot disappear when I am tired. I cannot ask for patience from someone else while failing to practise it myself. Accountability does not start in that way. It does not begin after something has already shifted, because by then the atmosphere is already in the room. It starts earlier, before the tightening in my chest becomes the tone of my voice, before that tone becomes something the other person has to respond to.

What I understand now is that the safety I wanted to create was never going to come from a single moment or a conversation that felt significant. It was going to come from consistency, the kind that holds across different conditions without needing reinforcement. A relationship should not feel like it needs to brace for one person's internal state, nor should it rely on cycles of disruption followed by repair to maintain its structure. Forgiveness has its place, and it remains necessary at times. Yet it should not become the mechanism that holds everything together, because when forgiveness becomes structural, it often signals that something is being repeated rather than resolved. I had to become someone who regulated himself before anyone had to ask, who saw his own shift and adjusted it before anyone had to point it out. Trust does not erode through singular events. It changes gradually, through repeated small inconsistencies left unaddressed, and I had left too many of mine unaddressed while telling myself the big things were what mattered.

Accountability also requires a refusal of entitlement, and this was an area where I had to be honest with myself about how easily responsibility in one part of life can be used to justify carelessness in another. Being capable at work, being consistent with external responsibilities, or carrying pressure well in one environment does not grant permission to relax discipline in another, because those areas are not separate in their effects. Pressure does not excuse tone, fatigue does not excuse dismissal, and stress does not excuse exporting internal strain into shared space. If something belongs to me, it remains mine to process, and it does not become someone else's atmosphere simply because they are close enough to feel it. Recognising that required a change in how I held what I was carrying, because it meant recognising that proximity does not create an obligation for another person to absorb what has not been managed internally.

Steadiness is different from endurance. Endurance carries pressure and holds. Steadiness absorbs it and keeps it from spreading outward, and that containment changes how others experience the environment. The version of me that builds something meaningful will not rely on apology as a repeated method of repair and will not depend on explanation after the fact to restore what has been disrupted. He will rely on awareness that reduces the need for repair in the first place, on noticing earlier, adjusting sooner, and maintaining alignment more consistently. That is not about removing mistakes or expecting perfection, because both are unrealistic. Yet it is about reducing the distance between awareness and correction, recognising when something has shifted, and returning to baseline before it becomes something larger.

The standard is not complicated. It is showing up the same way regardless of what the day did to me, so the person beside me does not have to work out which version of me walked through the door. That is, it. I do not want someone to have to read my face before deciding whether to bring something to me, or to assess whether tonight is a good night before saying what is on their mind. If you have ever watched someone you love hesitate before speaking because they were not sure how it would land, you know what that costs, and you know it is a cost that should not be there. The consistency must come from me regardless of the conditions, and that alignment is what allows something steady to exist without needing reinforcement.

Accountability is not a separate quality that can be added on top of everything else, but a continuous thread that runs through how I show up in every environment, because inconsistency between spaces does not stay contained within those spaces. The way I carry myself in one area influences how I carry myself in another, and any gap between what I value and how I act becomes more visible in closer proximity. That awareness has shifted how I think about readiness, because it is no longer defined by what I can handle, but by how consistently I can hold myself regardless of what I am handling. The posture is now less about proving anything and more about maintaining alignment, because what sustains connection over time is reliability in how I move through both pressure and presence.

Happiness After Grief

It arrives slowly, cautiously, and that hesitation feels right. In the preliminary stages of grief, even small moments of joy can feel disloyal, difficult to explain, because you laugh and then immediately feel the weight of memory, or you catch yourself smiling and question whether you are moving forward too quickly. I remember noticing that conflict inside myself, the way a light moment would be followed by a pull back toward what had been lost, and I had to learn that grief and happiness can sit in the same room without one erasing the other.

They can sit in the same room, and they can exist together without one pushing the other out, even though it takes time for that to feel natural.

What changed for me was not that the sadness disappeared, because it did not leave cleanly, with a clear before and after. It softened, and how it moved through everything else changed with it. It stopped sitting in my chest like something urgent that needed attention, and its edges dulled, less intrusive but not diminished. The memories became less sharp and more integrated, less likely to interrupt the present and more able to exist alongside it without taking over. I noticed this shift in ordinary moments, not the significant ones, in a genuine laugh that did not feel forced or followed by correction, in a conversation that flowed without heaviness attached to it, in a walk that felt like presence rather than an attempt to distract myself from what I was feeling. The laughter did not return all at once. It came back in fragments that settled quietly, and each time it returned, it stayed a little longer than before.

The mornings where I had a structure to follow were always better than the mornings where I did not. Wake up, drink water, run or train, shower, eat properly, sit for twenty minutes in quiet. Most mornings I wanted to stay in bed and let the day pass without me in it, and the structure carried me through those mornings, and on the other side of it I was always glad I had moved.

There was also a period where none of that was happening, and I need to acknowledge that because it was part of the process, though I did not fully understand it then. I sat still for longer than I needed to, I was eating poorly, I was not exercising, and the days blurred into each other. I told myself I just needed time. Sometimes that was true: there were moments where stopping and feeling was necessary and could not be avoided. What I did not see at first was that there is a point where being still stops helping and starts holding you in place, and I crossed that line without recognising it. The house was quiet in a way that sat heavy, my body felt flat, unable to move, and I told myself I just needed time, without questioning whether time alone was what was required. What I needed was motion, something to let what I was feeling move through me rather than settle.

The turning point was when I started moving again, because I knew what happened when I did not, and that knowledge was enough to begin. Exercise was different to how I had approached it before. It was not about fitness goals or outcomes. It gave my body somewhere to direct what it was holding. Running created a rhythm that let the tension move. Lifting steadied my thinking. Stand-up paddleboarding required balance and focus. Tennis and pickleball put me around people without heavy conversation, and the social side of it felt manageable in a way that other interactions did not. Movement interrupts the loop of internal focus. It is hard to stay in the same thought patterns when your body is working.

I want to say something about exercise that goes beyond how I used it through that period, because I think it gets treated as a tip when it is a foundation. I have loved movement my entire life, and that love did not start with grief. It was already there, already woven into how I operate, already the thing I came back to when everything else felt uncertain. What grief did was remind me of something I had let slide when I stopped prioritising it, which is that the body and the mind are not separate things and you cannot manage one without the other. When one is in disarray the other follows, and the reverse is also true. When I got moving again, things shifted in my thinking that sitting and reflecting had not been able to shift. The body carries what the mind cannot always get to through words, and movement reaches places that sitting and thinking do not.

Running is the one I come back to most, and

I always will. There is something in the bilateral rhythm of it, the left-right-left that moves through the body at a pace the nervous system seems to find regulating in a way nothing else quite replicates. I have run in the rain when I did not want to leave the house, and I have come back different. Not fixed. Not euphoric. Just quieter in a way I could feel in my body. I have run through periods where the only reason I went was that I knew what the day looked like when I did not, and that knowledge was always enough to get me out the door. That is what it became. Something I returned to before I felt ready because I knew what the day looked like when I did not.

Lifting does something different. It puts demand on the body that requires presence, because you cannot drift inside a set that is testing you. The focus is enforced, and that enforced focus pulls the mind into what is in front of you and away from the circular thinking. The tiredness from training hard is clean. The tiredness from sustained mental pressure is not, and my body learned to tell the difference across that period. One empties you in a way that asks for more. The other leaves you spent in a way that lets you rest.

I believe in exercise the way I believe in few other things. I believe it is one of the most underestimated tools available to anyone navigating a difficult part of their life, and I believe that most people who are carrying too much are also not moving enough, and that the two things are connected beyond the physical. You do not have to be a runner, and you do not have to lift weights. For me, easy wasn't enough. When the pressure was sitting high enough to affect my relationships, my body needed somewhere to put what it was holding, and that meant real demand. I kept coming back to that, consistently, without waiting to feel motivated. I am not running marathons and I am not an elite athlete. Exercise and losing weight and eating properly and prioritising all of it has made my body feel lighter, and that alone may have lowered my baseline more than I realise. None of that came easily. When I first got a personal trainer I wanted to vomit every session. I hated it. My mind would cycle through excuses for how I could get out of the next one before I had even arrived, and discipline was the only thing that carried me through that period because the motivation was nowhere. I was getting shin splints from running. My body was not used to the constant load. A year later my meniscus tore. The anxiety hit immediately because I knew surgery meant being still again, and I did not want that. The day after surgery I walked six kilometres. The surgeon advised that probably was not the best thing to do, but I knew that if I could get up the next day and move and stay disciplined, I would not treat that period as recovery and instead I would push forward. And that is what I did. My knee hurt for weeks afterwards, and I am not suggesting this was the right approach for anyone. I made a calculated decision based on my own history with movement and what I knew I needed. I do not recommend it as a template. You will always have setbacks, but doing things that are difficult builds character, and that sets a standard for your baseline.

It has taken a few years to get to a point where going to the gym or going for a run does not feel like a massive event. Back then I could feel the difference it made in a really pronounced way, like my body was grateful for the relief, like something had been wrung out of me that needed to go. Now it just feels normal, like something I do because I do it, and the feeling after is just a nice feeling, a happy feeling, nothing dramatic, simply good. I am not chasing anything when I walk in, and I am not recovering from anything when I walk out. My baseline does not crash and climb anymore. It just sits where it sits and the movement keeps it there, without any big moment attached to it, without me having to manufacture the motivation to get there because the motivation stopped being the point some time back. I just go. Mornings I would rather not and I go anyway, and it feels fine, and I come back and the day is the same day it would have been except something in my body settled without me having to manage it. That is what years of consistency gave me. It stops being something you do to feel better and becomes how you live, and the gap between those two things is bigger than I can explain to someone who has not been through it.

Music returned comparably, slowly and without intention beyond the act itself, and picking up the guitar was not about performance or improvement, but about rhythm and occupying space in my own mind without rumination. It gave structure to time that might otherwise have been spent repeating the same thoughts, and that structure created small breaks in patterns that had become familiar. Even my taste of music has slowly changed. When I was at my very lowest, music was sad, it was an outlet to get emotion out.

Look, if I still hear a sad song it pulls at the heart strings, but now I just enjoy music for what it is. I've gravitated from the slow sad melodies to just your everyday hot hit vibes. I think that's also a reflection of finding that happiness after grief. It's almost like a mirror of emotion. Things kept moving for me. I remember my grandmother told me once to live a happy life. I think once you experience loss and pain, the realisation of living happily is in the simple everyday things. It can be in your hobbies, your interests, the people you spend time with. It can be getting a coffee in the morning, breathing fresh air, listening to the rain of an evening. Not big events or a rollercoaster feeling that lasts for a few minutes, just the everyday moments that shape our lives. It's an important reflection I think, because once you start appreciating what you have, as opposed to what you don't have, that opens up a perspective that fulfills life. We may not be around forever, and it's naïve to think we will live to 100. Tomorrow isn't promised and neither are the years ahead. What I found when I started moving, my hobbies and interests started to come back. Investing, studying different courses, even the ones I did not complete, were not about achievement or completion, and instead were about engagement, about reminding myself that forward movement does not stop because something has ended. Drafting this book became part of that movement, as did journalling, because putting thoughts onto paper prevented them from circulating endlessly without resolution, and gave form to what had felt undefined.

Photography pulled me out of my own head. I had to look at what was in front of me, frame the shot, notice the light, pay attention to small details, and all of that widened my focus where grief had pulled it inward. Even following my football team more closely contributed in ways I had not expected, because it gave me something shared with other people that did not require vulnerability in the same way personal interactions did. There is something grounding about being part of a crowd, about being in moments that happen alongside other people without having to explain or process anything. That connection brought a different kind of rhythm back into my life. The funny thing is that happiness is addictive. My son could see me interested in sport again, and for the first time in his life, he wanted to watch it with me. And I think that's a beautiful thing to share with someone.

Socially, I had to be deliberate, and it did not feel natural at first, because grief makes isolation feel comfortable and justified, and it is easy to tell yourself that you will reconnect when you feel more like yourself. What I found was that waiting for that feeling often widened the distance, and I began to make a conscious effort to reach out to friends regularly, even when the interaction was simple and shallow. It was not about having significant conversations every time, nor about processing everything I was feeling in each interaction, but about maintaining connection in ways that felt manageable. Sometimes it was just banter; sometimes it was a meeting to play, train, or share an activity, and those moments reinforced that I was still part of something, even when I did not feel expansive.

Sitting remains important, and reflection continues to matter, yet I learned that it cannot be the only approach, because without movement, things settle in ways that are difficult to shift. Emotional movement, physical movement, and social movement all play a part in keeping grief from settling into something permanent, and none of them is optional if you want to come through it. Motivation does not always arrive first. I had to accept that. Moving before I felt ready was often what brought the readiness back. It is not about distraction. It is about circulation. When you stay still too long what you are holding hardens, and movement softens it.

Happiness after grief feels different to what came before. The quality of it has changed: less dependent on external reinforcement, not needing intensity to feel real, sitting in a steadier place that does not fluctuate in the same way. There is less urgency attached to it and less fear of losing it, which changes is how it is experienced, since it does not need to be held on to tightly. Moments are allowed to exist without being gripped, and that shift creates a unique way of moving through the world, one not driven by the avoidance of pain.

Being ready for love again and not needing it to feel complete turned out to be the same thing, and that changed how I saw the space I was in. There was a time when I would have looked to fill that space quickly, to soften discomfort by introducing something new, yet now the absence of a relationship feels less like something missing and more like something available. That space is active rather than empty, filled with discipline, movement, interests, conversations, and movement that does not depend on anyone else to exist. I am not rushing to fill it, and I am not trying to accelerate what comes next, because the steadiness of that space is what shows me I am ready, not through urgency for connection, but through the ability to offer it without needing it to stabilise me.

There are still moments when grief returns, recognisable, often triggered by something small and unexpected, a song, a memory, an evening that carries a familiar tone, yet those moments no longer disrupt the structure of how I feel. The feeling moves through and settles without expanding. I do not interpret it as longing or as a sign that something is unresolved, but as an indication that something mattered deeply enough to remain present. That presence does not interfere with what exists now; instead, it becomes part of it, part of it and not separate from it.

Happiness now feels grounded, difficult to describe without experiencing it, and it carries a sense of having been built rather than found. It feels earned. I laugh more easily now, and I move through the day without scanning for what might shift. Silence feels like peace rather than relief, and the safety in it does not need the day to have gone well to be there.

I don't know who I will love next or when that will happen, and that uncertainty does not create urgency in the way it once might have, because whoever I am when that moment comes will not be defined by what he is trying to recover or replace. He will be moving, engaged, regulated, and connected. Not trying to recreate what has passed or escape it. Carrying it so something new can form cleanly. Grief reshaped me in ways I did not expect, movement steadied me in ways I could not have forced, and happiness came back because I kept going long enough for it to settle in its own time. It is all I could do, keep going. And I'm so glad that I did.

Love Isn't Finite

There is another layer to this that matters, and it is not spoken about enough, because it sits beneath how people approach connection and often shapes it without being named directly. Just because I have loved before does not dilute what love can become again, and it took time for that to feel like something I could stand in without qualification. The fact that something once mattered deeply does not take anything away from what is possible next, even though it is easy to think emotional investment has limits or that meaning fades with repetition. Love looks different depending on where you are in your life, and it changes shape depending on what you have been through. When it was real, it was real, and that truth does not require adjustment to make anything that follows feel more secure.

My children are the clearest evidence of that. The love I carry for my daughter does not compete with the love I carry for my son. My son showed me I had more patience in me than I knew. My daughter showed me that love can exist across distance and still be fierce. Every person I have loved has changed me and every one of them has made me more capable of loving the next.

Some people become cautious about admitting that, and I understand why, because there is a vulnerability in acknowledging that something in the past held weight, especially when standing in the possibility of something new. They soften the language and call what they felt confusion or immaturity, so it does not feel like it carries forward. They say it "wasn't really love" because that feels safer, because it removes the need to hold two truths at once, and it avoids comparison, and it avoids discomfort. It avoids the exposure that comes with admitting that someone else once mattered in a significant way. But denying something genuine does not create a stronger foundation for what comes next, nor does it make a new connection more secure. It weakens the foundation in ways that are not always immediately visible, because if you are willing to rewrite your own history to make someone comfortable, you are signalling that truth is negotiable. That negotiation does not stay contained to the past.

Loving someone in the past does not compete with loving someone in the future, and it does not create a ranking where one has to be smaller for the other to feel real. It shows what you are capable of in a way that words alone cannot, because it shows you can open fully and commit and move into something that carries real weight. Pretending you never felt deeply might protect your pride but it ruins the foundation. It makes you look safer but it makes you smaller, and that limits what you can build from there. The truth is simpler and stronger than that, even if it feels more exposed, because being able to say that I have loved before and been open before does not take anything away from what comes next. It allows it to exist with greater awareness, greater intention, and a clearer understanding of what it means to hold something.

Every person carries a history, whether they speak about it directly or not, and every person has chapters that shaped how they see connection, how they respond to it, and how they move within it. You do not have to erase those parts of your life to be mature. What happened does not go away just because you stop talking about it. What matters is not whether love existed before, and it is not whether something ended, but whether it is carried honestly into the present without distortion. Love can exist fully in one part of your life and still end and still have meant something, and it can be right for a season and not need to last forever to count. It can evolve, and it can fracture, and it can teach in ways that are not immediately clear while you are inside it, and none of that cancels its authenticity or reduces what it was when it existed.

If someone feels threatened by the truth that you have loved before, the problem is not the past. It is what they are feeling now. The past only becomes a problem when they see it as competing with what is happening now. Foundations are built on clarity. They hold when you can stand in what has been without reshaping it and bring that into what you are building. When you deny your own emotional history you do not become more loyal or committed. You do not create greater security for the other person either. You become less trustworthy because if you can dismiss what was once real, people start to wonder whether what is happening now could also be dismissed when it gets uncomfortable.

It existed in the form it needed to, shaped by who you were and what you understood and what you could hold. The next version will look different because you are not the same person, and what you bring into it carries greater awareness, steadiness, and understanding of what matters. It will carry lessons I have actually learned instead of repeated, and it will move at a different pace because you are no longer relying on the same patterns to define it. But it will not require erasing what came before to exist fully, because what happened becomes part of how you move forward and not something you have to cut out.

The truth grounds you when you hold it clearly, and it weakens when you adjust it to fit what feels more comfortable. Being able to say that you have loved deeply before is not a liability. It does not weaken what you can build in the future. It proves you can do depth and presence and that you can open to something that matters. That capacity does not disappear when something ends, nor does it diminish over time, and standing in that truth without softening it is part of what allows the next chapter to be built without distortion.

I do not hide the fact that I have loved before, and I do not intend to. Those relationships were real. They mattered. And the fact that they ended does not reduce what they were, or what I am capable of carrying into what comes next. I am not carrying damage from that into something new. I am carrying awareness. That capacity is intact. If anything, it is clearer.

If you have ever caught yourself downplaying something that mattered, softening the language around someone you loved because it felt easier than standing in the truth of it, this is what I am talking about. The maturity is not in moving past what was real. It is in being honest about it without needing permission, and in knowing that the capacity to love deeply is not something that gets used up. It is something you carry with you.

Home

Being steady took me time to recognise, because I had expected something more obvious, something that would clearly signal that I had crossed into a different place. I thought peace would feel like a moment, something distinct and noticeable, like a weight being lifted all at once, like everything that had been heavy would drop cleanly and stay there. I imagined a shift that would separate what had been from what is, something I could point to and say, "That was when it changed." It has not been that and learning to accept that has been part of the process, because what replaced it did not arrive with the same clarity or force. It has been ordinary, easy to overlook if you are still looking for something dramatic, a series of mornings where I wake. My chest is not already holding tension, evenings that end without unwinding what the day did to me, just a sense of completion that does not ask for anything more. I am still responsible, and I still carry weight, and life did not become lighter in the way I once thought it might, yet something fundamental shifted in how I hold it, because I stopped carrying it with my shoulders raised, and that change created space where there had only been pressure.

I used to treat being alone and being unsettled as the same thing. I would fill silence quickly because it felt wrong to sit in it. I used to think silence was something I needed to manage, something to fill with noise or activity so I did not have to sit in it too long. I would reach for something without thinking, to avoid that stillness, because it felt wrong instead of feeling like something I could sit in. Now it feels like space I can sit inside without reaching for anything. I can make dinner without anything playing in the background, though it is nice to have music on whilst cooking. I can drive and not need to fill the time. I can lie in bed and not rehearse tomorrow, and those moments no longer feel like something is missing. They feel complete as they are, and that changes how I move through time, because I am no longer pushing toward the next thing to make it feel full.

Sadness still arrives, and I still miss her, and not in any way that suggests resolution or replacement, yet it no longer moves through everything else in the same way. I can feel it without it pulling everything down, and I can sit with it without interpreting it as something that will unravel me. I can feel something now without being taken over by it, and that has become clearer over time. I can miss someone and not lose myself in it, and I can feel grief and not turn it into collapse.

You feel it before you can name it, carrying it better. You know when you are doing it and you know when you are not, and the people around you know before you do. It is about showing up as yourself, present and honest, not somewhere else in your head while the people you love are right in front of you. That is the standard. And a standard only means something when you carry it into the room with you, when it sits on you like something you chose, something you are accountable for. That is what this is. That is what carry it better means.

I have not been in a relationship since everything changed, and that is not because I closed myself off or stepped away from connection. I understood I was not ready to bring what I had been carrying into something new. I did not want to bring urgency disguised as chemistry, or to confuse intensity with depth again, and I was aware enough to know that if I did not change that baseline, I would repeat the same patterns with a different person. It would look different on the surface, but it would carry the same underlying tension, and I did not want that anymore. So, I stayed where I was. I was clear about why. I was letting things settle before I tried to build something else on top of them.

I also did not want loneliness to be the thing that moved me toward someone. That felt like the wrong reason, and I have seen what it produces, what happens when two people find each other at exactly the wrong moment and mistake the relief of company for something deeper. I wanted to come to whatever is next from a place that was already full. Not looking to be completed or steadied or distracted from what I was still carrying. There is a version of me that would have moved quickly toward someone just to have somewhere to put all of that, and I know that version well enough to know I did not want to be him again.

Once, I would have mistaken urgency for connection and relief for love, and I understand now how easy that confusion is when everything is running at an elevated pace. Intensity feels powerful because it is loud and immediate and consuming. It gives the impression that something significant is happening because you feel it so strongly. It creates movement, and that movement can feel like progress even when it is not. Depth does not work that way. It does not need force to be real. It does not rush or demand or depend on tension. It stays. Your body settles in it and you can stay there without bracing for it to change. You can live in it. You do not have to hold it together.

It came from repetition, from lowering the baseline, from staying in moments where I used to tighten, from recognising that responsibility includes the tone of your voice and the atmosphere you create, and from adjusting those things consistently rather than occasionally. It came from paying attention to how I moved through ordinary situations. From noticing when I was leaning forward. From stepping back into what was actually there.

It is capacity. It is knowing that if love comes, it will meet someone who can hold it without bracing and without trying to manage it. Not braced. Not scanning. Not a man trying to outrun his own nervous system. Someone who can stay present without trying to manage what is happening. I do not want intensity anymore in the way I once did. I want presence. I want depth. I want something steady that does not need me to hold it up. I am also a realist, and I understand that love may never arrive again. I am comfortable with that. What I had was real, and if love does come again, I can meet it differently now.

I am not finished, and I do not think anyone ever is, yet I am no longer living in a state of elevation, and that changes how everything moves through me.

And if love arrives again, it will meet me as I am. I think that counts for something.

Acknowledgements

To everyone who helped me through all of it, thank you. To the professionals who supported me. To the friends and family who listened without trying to fix. To the people who gently challenged me. To those who gave me space when I needed it.

To my children who kept me going on my toughest days.

About the Author

E.J. Ellsworth spent over a decade in high-pressure environments where responsibility was constant and the margin for error was small. After years of carrying that weight without knowing how to regulate, the cost became impossible to ignore. It showed up in his relationships, in the distance between who he wanted to be and who kept arriving under pressure, and eventually in the fractures that followed.

What came after was the slow, unglamorous work of rebuilding, learning to carry responsibility, heartbreak, and the love that remained.

Through lived experience, personal study, and professional support, he developed a practical approach to emotional capacity, grounded in awareness, regulation, discipline, and presence.

He is a dedicated father of two beautiful children and continues to focus on building a steadier, more present way of moving through life.

Further Reading

The works below are offered as further reading for those who wish to explore the research and thinking that sit beneath many of the ideas discussed.

Ainsworth, Mary; Blehar, Mary; Waters, Everett; and Wall, Sally. *Patterns of Attachment: A Psychological Study of the Strange Situation.*

Bowlby, John. *Attachment and Loss: Volume 1, Attachment.*

Craske, Michelle; Treanor, Michelle; Conway, Catherine; Zbozinek, Timothy; and Vervliet,

Bram. "Maximizing Exposure Therapy: An Inhibitory Learning Approach." *Behaviour Research and Therapy.*

Goleman, Daniel. *Emotional Intelligence.*

Goode, William. "A Theory of Role Strain." *American Sociological Review.*

Gross, James; and Thompson, Ross. "Emotion Regulation: Conceptual Foundations." In *Handbook of Emotion Regulation.*

McEwen, Bruce; and Lasley, Elizabeth. *The End of Stress as We Know It.*

Mikulincer, Mario; and Shaver, Phillip. *Attachment in Adulthood.*

Neff, Kristin. *Self-Compassion.*

Porges, Stephen. *The Polyvagal Theory.*

Sapolsky, Robert. *Why Zebras Don't Get Ulcers.*

Schore, Allan. *Affect Regulation and the Origin of the Self.*

Siegel, Daniel. *The Developing Mind.*

Sterling, Peter; and Eyer, Joseph. "Allostasis: A New Paradigm to Explain Arousal Pathology."

In *Handbook of Life Stress, Cognition and Health.*

van der Kolk, Bessel. *The Body Keeps the Score.*

Worden, William. *Grief Counselling and Grief Therapy.*

www.ingramcontent.com/pod-product-compliance
Lightning Source LLC
Chambersburg PA
CBHW032005050726
47590CB00006B/2051

9781764643399